What others are saying ab

Exercise your faith muscle...

Adventure, intrigue, inspiration, and curiosity grabbed my attention and didn't let go until the end. Catch Your Breath is a legacy book that you will want your children and grandchildren to read. Linda's words are convicting, thought provoking and will challenge you to exercise your faith muscle. Read it slowly and participate in the suggested activities. Every chapter is scriptural truth lived out through Linda's experiences in Africa, which whet one's appetite for more. This book will become a reference book to return to time and time again.

Tammy Lollar, Spiritual Mentor

Escape your own long-occupied ruts...

The waves of unending busyness in most of our lives keep us languishing in a sea of spiritual barrenness. Catch Your Breath is like an energizing drink of cool, fresh water to a thirsty, desert-parched spirit. If you have yearned to escape your own long-occupied ruts and revive your passion for God's presence, you will be delighted to embark on an unhurried, deliberate journey with this book. You will find conviction, encouragement, and a clearly marked pathway to a daily, personal experience of God's grace and goodness.

Dr. Tim Hight, Senior Pastor GraceLife Baptist Church, Christiansburg, VA

A glimpse of how God works...

Let the power of God use this book to open your heart and eyes to better understand God's kingdom agenda, His ways, and His purpose for you. Understanding and applying the truths from God's Word shared in Catch Your Breath will encourage and energize you to live with intentionality with a glimpse of how God works in refreshing, thought provoking ways. Many amazing God stories reflect the depth of Linda's love for God's Word, prayer, and serving others. The result is a powerful personal testimony of God's grace, mercy, and love that will entice you to taste and see that the Lord is good!

James Lollar, Phd, Professor and Chair, Radford University

Ah Ha moments...

Linda shares so many Ah Ha moments of her life. The book is a treasure of a life of service to our Lord, Jesus Christ, leading the reader to a deeper commitment of his/her life. May God receive all the glory.

Maggi Jones, Serves in prayer ministry and elder guardianship

Relevant in this chaotic world...

If you've lost the AWE and WONDER of our creator, then read this book. The author shares stories from her 30 missionary years in Africa. The message is just as relevant in this chaotic world we live in today. My heart has been uplifted and encouraged. It reminds me of how God is in the details of our daily lives. Will be reading over and over to get all the good nuggets I missed the first time around.

Melissa Coleman, Student of the Word

Joys and humor that sustain...

The wonder and majesty of God's love for His chosen is the focus of this lovely book of a missionary couple's journey in Uganda. We share the frights that build faith, the joys and humor that sustain, and the aha moments that move us closer in our walk with God. Linda helps us to understand how we are chosen, cherished, protected and important in God's Plan for His Creation, and how knowing that helps us to live freer, fuller, and more fruitfully. The wonder of it all makes us hungry for more of the little details and surprises in our journey with God as our eyes open to His long-term plan for our lives and for His Creation.

Cheryl Downey, Advocate for troubled children in the courts

A road map to...opportunities...

This book reveals through everyday events the tapestry of a life lived with purpose for Christ. In her writing she shows that walking in faith is an adventure. The author has given us a road map to help us be more aware of the opportunities in our own lives to experience God. Hands up!

Bob and Donna Barbetti, Disciple-makers

CATCH YOUR BREATH!

prepare to leave the rut...

Linda Rice

Catch Your Breath

Contents

Catch Your Breath

African Lessons

You were taught, with regard to your former way of life,
to put off your old self... and to put on the new self,

Ephesians 4:22, 24

Church in Africa—our first Sunday! Packed shoulder to shoulder, we sat in the center of a long, narrow, wooden bench. The window shutters opened wide, drums set the beat for singing, and a bell rang to limit the length of testimonies, so that all had a chance to speak. Before the sermon even began, I realized I hadn't dressed properly. All the children, from youngest to oldest, formed a line, and worked their way past the knees of worshipers on our bench. They stopped at me, briefly rubbed my legs, and moved on to the other end of the row. This white woman's legs with their unusual texture were a compelling attraction. That morning, I decided to discard a piece of my American culture—my nylon hose.

* * *

My husband, Jim, and I left Virginia in 1975, to work as missionaries in East Africa. We settled into Mbale, the third largest town in Uganda. Uganda's president, Idi Amin, began his rule in 1971, when he orchestrated a military coup, grasping control of the nation. The population rejoiced at the overthrow of the former leader and his oppressive methods. However, Amin's honeymoon period soon ended, as he relentlessly devastated the economy, medical services, and any sense of safety. He expelled Asian and African entrepreneurs, removed his traditional tribal enemies from positions of prominence including students from the university, and he oversaw the death of thousands of Ugandans. By 1974, the world beyond Uganda's borders had heard of Amin's reign of terror and atrocity. Under the influence of Libya's strongman leader Muammar Gaddafi, restrictions increased curtailing Christian activity. As these restrictions grew more intense, missionaries left the country.

So why, in 1975, did this government grant Jim a permit to live and work in Uganda? Considering the collapse of the medical community, our mission applied for a work permit for a physician, which received a quick rejection despite the great need. The rejection stated that Uganda could take care of its medical needs. Yet, Jim's application, listing a business education background, garnered a welcome approval. It made no sense from man's perspective, yet God must have thought otherwise.

Jim entered Uganda to serve as business manager and treasurer for the Baptist Mission, which consisted of only two other families, in 1975. In addition, and perhaps foremost, we did whatever we could to encourage pastors and churches to stand strong for Christ. We were two young, naïve twenty-eight-year-olds. We spent our next twenty-eight years in this unpredictable land. God provided a steady stream of training exercises and lessons, equipping us for the task. Many of these lessons involved *putting off* former ways and *putting on* new ways.

One of the more troublesome lessons to master involved timekeeping. Ugandans don't keep time. Jim struggled with this pervasive lack of punctuality. More than once, he drove three hours to meet with immigration officials in the capital, Kampala, only to learn that, "The man with the key to the desk has not yet appeared. Come back tomorrow!"

Schedules merely set the order of progression but said little regarding the when.

Everyone wanted a watch, perhaps for accessorizing, as it certainly wasn't to know the time. After thieves stole the third watch off my arm, I quit wearing one, thereby liberating me from that bit of daily stress, allowing me to go with the flow. This *putting off* the former ways of timekeeping enabled me to live well within God's assignment in Uganda.

Actually, as time progressed, even though it wasn't kept, we discovered the underlying principle worth *putting on*. People take priority. If you meet a friend along the way, you stop for conversation. If someone appears at your door, you invite him in and give him a cup of tea, even if you have an appointment elsewhere. When someone falls sick and needs a ride to the hospital, you go. Best friends come unannounced, so that it's okay to have no prepared food to offer. You lead a Bible study in which questions keep arising. The allotted time ends. Why shouldn't you answer now, rather than delay until next week, even if it takes another hour or two?

God gives us this day and these people. Tomorrow has not yet come. People take precedence over schedule, and this time is more compelling than that which is not yet here. Both lessons have a biblical ring to them, good lessons to put on. Nonetheless, for me, whose dad counted me late unless I arrived at least ten minutes early, this lesson proved a difficult addition. I might never have learned "the people take priority over time" lesson in Virginia.

God found Uganda an excellent training field for another lesson, his perspective on safety—including the possibility of death. Eight military coups provided opportunities to rest our lives fully in the hands of the Lord. During the 1986 coup, the outgoing army held the hill above us and the incoming army advanced through the valley below us. Both armies fired mortars over our house, causing curtains to billow and creating waves in the waterbed. Jim, Kristen our two-year old daughter, and I huddled in the hallway. Ten others, some visitors and some strangers passing by the house as fighting began, huddled with us. We recorded the blasts and booms of that event on a cassette tape. In the midst of the recording, you hear "pass the peanut butter down this way." As the chaos of war raged outside, we did pray, but also we ate and enjoyed each other in the hallway, resting in the Lord. I have several enormous brass shell casings from that event. We use them as flower vases to remind us of God's peace in the midst of strife.

Soldiers manning road checks creatively reinforced this lesson. At one road check, a soldier ordered me to leave the vehicle, as he spotted a road map on the seat. He was convinced that the presence of a map identified me as a CIA spy. Vigorous discussion with the Lord consumed my mind and heart, as I stood for thirty minutes on that hot dusty road, before they released me to continue the journey! Another reinforcement lesson came through Angie, the six-year-old child of a missionary colleague. She taught us, as she declared that she would sleep peacefully despite the loud, violent sounds and screams of a military incursion in our neighborhood. "Don't you see that the window frames make a shadow of a big cross on top of my bed? I'm under the cross." Another memorable night, gunfire erupted all around our Kampala neighborhood. Peeking out the window, Jim checked on the whereabouts of our guard. The guard, on his hands and knees, felt around the ground—he had dropped his one bullet. Images of Barney Fife in Mayberry sprang to mind. "Let's go back to sleep, Linda. Obviously, the Lord protects this house, and not this guard we've hired!"

God provided abundant teaching and testing opportunities to stretch and mature our faith. I learned to carry my stuff in my hands and not in my heart. We lost count of the robberies, from multiple automobile hijackings to overnight guests taking Jim's shoes. God used a variety of teaching tools. Mayinja, a friend who worked with our mission in high school student ministries, asked if he could come to the house to discuss a spiritual matter. He feared this issue indicated a weakening of his walk with the Lord. Why? When he had two pairs of trousers, he could readily give away one to a person in need. Now that he had four pair, he found it difficult to let go of even one. Who taught and who learned? God's lessons can run both directions simultaneously.

Other more complicated lessons took time to get right, and required frequent retraining. Obedience in this present moment is *the* issue regardless of great or small obedience in the past or any promised obedience for the future. Later I'll tell you a story of a small obedience when a payment for one can of green beans yielded four hundred boiled eggs. God's ways differ from our ways. Months of prayer for spiritual awakening can find fulfillment amid an AIDS pandemic. Who would have thought! God will use whomever he chooses. You'll read the Zawedde story in a later chapter. After twenty-five years in Uganda and three in Kenya, we returned to Virginia in 2003. Reorientation and reflection filled our minds. We weren't the same people who left Virginia. Some days we felt as foreign in this land as we had in Uganda. Once again, the process commenced to determine what I must discard, what I should keep, and which lessons needed a retrofit for our new locality.

Our Virginian sense of decorum fell away as we grew to love the African vigor in worship—clapping, dancing, shouting, and even marching around the building occasionally. Back in Christiansburg, we reluctantly reigned in exuberance. As temperatures dropped, I regretfully wore hose again. The American arm's length of personal space disappeared in Africa. One more person could always fit in a vehicle, on the church pew, or around our dining table. Two people sharing a chair worked, if only one chair was available. If we tried that here, we'd risk censure. I've learned that no one appreciates drop-in visits. When someone says ten o'clock, he means ten o'clock. Neither my eggs nor my ears of corn fit the church's offering plate. It's highly unlikely that I will ever change another Nissan van fuel filter due to dirty petrol. Nor is it likely that I will use my well-honed skill to receive the gift of a live chicken graciously. Much we learned in Uganda is not helpful in Virginia.

At the same time, some Uganda-learned lessons I don't want to lose, such as holding stuff in my hands and not my heart, giving priority to people, and making the most of the time in this day. Reminiscing through those African years, one lesson does stand out, dominating the big picture. God's people can be in the right place, at the right time, doing the right thing—consistently. This lesson applies just as well in Virginia as it did in Africa. Not only have I determined to hold it undimmed in my life but also I long for others to believe it, embrace it, and live it. This wondrous truth leads us to live on the same page as God. He is just as likely to show up at any time in American as he did during our missionary career in Uganda. I shall attempt to convince you to believe this truth, and then I want to show you how it works. First, let me tell you a story.

Bundibugyo, Uganda 1975

Bundibugyo, (Boo-endi-boo-joe), a district on Uganda's remote western border with Congo, held several churches. Due to the scarcity of transportation and the arduous nature of the journey, these churches rarely received visitors. In 1975, one main road, only fifteen percent paved and frequently flooded, circled the huge swamp of Lake Kyoga, which comprised the center of the country. We planned a trip to take the pastors of Mbale to visit and preach in the churches of Bundibugyo to strengthen and encourage them. Several months ahead, we sent multiple letters stating our intentions and the date of our arrival, asking someone to meet us at the government district office to lead us to the churches. We hoped and prayed that at least one of the letters would arrive before we did. No reply came back to us. Nevertheless, we went.

Bundibugyo lay in a valley on the backside of the Ruwenzori Mountains of the Moon, a snow capped rugged range with exotic flora. One precariously narrow, rock-strewn, pot-holed, dirt road winds from Fort Portal thirty miles around the mountain. You could drive upwards east on it in the mornings and downwards west in the afternoons. Our assigned vehicle, a van neither skinny nor four-wheel-drive, made this a white-knuckle, breath-taker of a journey. Arriving at the bottom with great thankfulness, we found steaming pools of water due to the volcanic nature of the mountains. This lush land, with a National Geographic quality impenetrable rain forest of towering trees and dark recesses, had a tantalizing air of mystery and danger. Pygmies, who lived and hunted in the forest, practiced witchcraft. They grew a few crops, including opium, in sunlit clearings.

When we reached the district office, a man, standing in the courtyard, watching for our vehicle, welcomed us. We celebrated, as this meant our letter had arrived. With only a few hours of daylight left, we quickly proceeded to drop pastors at their host churches. Leaving the road, we drove along footpaths into the forest. Each church welcomed their guest pastor with great festivity, then we hustled away to find the next church.

The last church, a number of miles down a steep incline, posed a challenge. By the time we were ready to leave, darkness and dew had fallen, making the grasses along the footpath wet and slippery. Our van now held only three occupants, Jim, our local guide, and me, making it quite lightweight. If we hoped to reach the top of that steep incline, we had to start as fast as possible and keep moving. Unfortunately, the grass hid a stump. We hit it with the jarring shock of a blowout, and abruptly halted. Jim crawled under the vehicle with a flashlight. In the thick darkness of the forest, I fired up the Coleman lantern for more light, and held it above Jim's head. Not only did we have a burst tire but also Jim found a bent tie rod. To relieve the stress of the day, I stretched my neck, twisting my head—I was stunned. On the outer rim of the lantern's circle of light, elbow to elbow, stood short men, scantily dressed, holding bows with arrows.

I hadn't heard them come, and certainly, Jim was unaware of their presence. I tried to tell him, but I couldn't seem to take my eyes off this circle of men to turn towards Jim, or to voice any recognizable sound. The lantern in my hand seriously shook. The only coherent thought in my mind was, *if my mother could see me now!* Did I tell you that pygmies hunt with poison tipped arrows?

I finally stammered, "Look up," and Jim stood. What an unbelievable predicament! We might as well relax, as clearly, the only one who could possibly handle this situation was the Lord. These men couldn't speak to us, and we couldn't speak with them. Even our local guide could not, as this small district had several languages. Warily, and with curiosity, we watched each other until I doused the lamp. We got into the van and settled, with no way to move and nowhere to go. Eventually, the pygmies, with their bows and arrows, melted into the darkness. As light arrived, we awoke—yes, we did sleep. Also with the first rays of dawn, a sizeable group of short men arrived again, this time with long ropes. Tying them together and onto the car, the whole host of them pulled us up the path to the road and pushed us the entire distance to the district office. After pitching our tent on the district office's lawn, we spent the week. By the time we left, the tire and tie rod were repaired, another story in itself.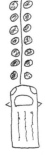

The meetings went well with unexpected large attendance. The entire region, every deep recess of the forest, heard of our presence. Even the most successful New York ad agency couldn't have designed a more effective campaign to publicize these revival meetings, as God did with our night of the bent tie rod.

* * *

The truth God proved—over and over—during our African years is that *God's people can be in the right place, at the right time, doing the right thing—consistently.* I suspect many of you do not believe this. I pray that as I share lessons God taught us, your doubt will change to confidence, and confidence will move into practice.

From the first instance of our existence to the last,

God has never assigned us a barren moment.[1]

Francois Fénelon, French writer 1651-1715

Another 1975 Story

A few months after our arrival in Mbale, a Ugandan pastor asked me to take him and several church members to a gathering in another church. This event, located fifty miles around the backside of Mt. Elgon, would take two hours, as the region was quite rural with minimal roads. The night before departure it rained—an important fact. We packed the Land Rover with more people than I thought possible. Remember that I'm still a newbie to Africa. Halfway into the journey, we slogged through a section of black-cotton soil, dirt blacker and stickier than any soil I had ever seen. With the steep incline of the mountain and the weight of the passengers, I couldn't get enough speed out of the aging Land Rover to traverse the muck. This patch had absorbed the previous night's downpour, creating a suction, which wouldn't be denied. We sank and stuck. A short distance ahead, another Land Rover sat mired in that mud.

Our men took off shoes, rolled up pants legs, and went to join their push. I too got out, but eyeing that black ooze, I kept on my tennis shoes. I looked for a spot to apply my muscle, and stepped into a small gap between two men. We huffed, we puffed, and suddenly the vehicle lurched forward with a loud *shmuck*, as the suction broke, freeing the wheel. I was shocked—not that the vehicle popped out of the rut—but that the spinning wheel, right in front of me, spewed a tire-wide slather of muck from my feet to the top of my head. Everyone else knew not to stand directly behind the tire. Thankfully, this time, I was only the driver and not a speaker. I had much to learn!

The Premise

I chose you and appointed you to go and bear fruit.

John 15:16

Have you had those moments when the Lord's presence was so palpable your skin tingles? Events flowed in such a way that God's orchestration was obvious. Coincidence couldn't have been responsible for such an outcome. Exciting? For sure! We can recite the details, as they are etched in our memory. We speak them in testimony to God's love for us, his involvement in the lives of his children, an extraordinary meeting of a need, or a surprisingly profitable turn of events. We've had those delicious instances of powerful oneness of spirit in worship when we knew that the Spirit of the Lord dwelt with us. We don't want them to end. Those Spirit-infused times, as we soar in prayer to heights previously unknown, thrill us. We've had those encounters, which seemed random on the surface but in retrospect, demonstrate that actually God arranged that meeting, that comment or that act. Someone troubled and needy experienced God's calming, healing touch. So much accomplished with so little effort on our part!

Those moments are rare! Why do these God-encounters appear so seldom? The rarity of such times troubles my spirit. An even greater irritant is the fact that we believe this rarity to be God's design. I've peered at this from many angles. I've examined the Bible, read excellent books, and studied histories of the saints. I've prayed, talked, and tested. As I pursued an answer, the irritating question began to act as a grain of sand for my soul. This grain of sand in the Lord's hands has further transformed into a pearl within my life, which excites me.

I want to share this excitement with you, to display this pearl for your inspection. It isn't new or original, yet it is wondrous. Many others have written on God's desire to walk closely with his people every day. So why do I add yet another book to the shelf? The Lord's activity in my life is unique just as his activity in your life is unique. Perhaps something from my journey will ignite a spark in your life. Perhaps one of my *Ah Ha!* moments will help some of your puzzling pieces snap into place.

I firmly believe as the French believer Fénelon said long ago, "God has never assigned us a barren moment," not even one. He isn't a God of barrenness. Not only has he designed every moment to be fruitful, he has filled it with an astounding bounty of fruitfulness. God, the supreme multitasker, works in myriad directions, on myriad issues, through myriad persons, within every moment of the day. In *Experiencing God,* Henry Blackaby teaches that God longs for us to join him in kingdom activity, even waits for us to do so. God loves to affirm and confirm us along the way, even to the point of a skin-tingling and chest-tightening, *knowing* that we are in the same spot as he, experiencing precisely what he has designed.

We, God's people in whom Jesus Christ resides, can live in the right place, at the right time, doing the right thing—consistently. Living in sync with God's design is our wondrous Christ-secured expectation for everyday, for this day.

Os Guiness, in *The Call*, wrote, "Calling is the truth that God calls us to himself so decisively that everything we are, everything we do, and everything we have is invested with a special devotion and dynamism lived out as a response to his summons and service."[2] I plan to address that *dynamism*, a vigorous tangible dynamism, which envelopes and permeates our lives, as we respond to Jesus's summons to "Follow me" (Matthew 4:19). Join me, as we examine this pearl, holding it up for scrutiny, catching its iridescence and luster as light reflects in multiple directions.

I will use every opportunity to share our African stories for illustration. And you will discover I love the images and visions of Zechariah. Zechariah was God's prophet to the small, sorely disillusioned, band of Israelites who after seventy years of Babylonian captivity returned to find their beloved Jerusalem burnt to the ground. God gave these visions to encourage and guide his people through this dire situation. So, you might as well get your Bible now and locate his book. As Ugandans say, it is the "last but one" in the Old Testament. You will see that I ask many questions. Please read with pen and paper, even a notebook, in hand. Jot down your immediate reactions for further reflection. They could be from the Lord, and Satan can snatch them so quickly.

You could read this short book quickly. Please do not. If you skim the text, the words will travel through your mind and, before long, out of your memory. They will not soak down into your heart and soul. I have spiced these pages with activities that I hope will provide for a deeper soak. When I ask you to stand up, buy apples, stick a cowboy picture on your mirror or work a jigsaw puzzle, please take time to do it. A deadline hasn't been set. Speed isn't a spiritual virtue. Most importantly, read the Bible verses for yourself. I have not written them for you, so you will have to use a Bible. Weak disciples wait for others to tell them what God's Word says. Verify all I write by checking the Scriptures. This doesn't waste your time. There is no better marinade for your life than the Word of God. Such an unhurried soak tenderizes you toward God and flavors life with his divine efficiency. Consider the alternative. What flavor does life acquire after months or years of running in busy frantic circles? A hardness toward others, exhaustion, or simply disappointment with rarely finishing the to-do list? Proceed slowly.

We can live in the right place, at the right time, doing the right thing—consistently. God has written an agenda for this day. He waits for us to get on the same page. No doubt twists and turns will come. God doesn't move in a single, straight line. No doubt, Satan will tell you that you don't have what it takes. The continuous flow of the Spirit says otherwise.

Today's Agenda

This is the day the Lord has made; let us rejoice and be glad in it.

Psalm 118:24

It is not an agenda designed only for pastors and super-Christians.

It's for all whose eyes are looking toward God, who follow him.

It's for everyone, not looking to God, who is walking away from him.

Comprehensive

It is not the broad strokes of a vague idea, a general direction plan.

It is precise, creative beyond our wildest imaginations.

There is an agenda for my life and your life today.

Detailed

It is not an agenda activated only on Sundays or other holy days.

It's not suspended as sin-levels reach three on a scale of ten.

Unexpected circumstances cannot disrupt or derail it.

Often the unexpected is his plan.

Current-for-This-Moment

It is not an agenda drafted with limited knowledge.

It is a plan fully aware of the sin-prone actors chosen for the task.

"I know the plans I have for you," (Jeremiah 29:11).

"The Lord Almighty has purposed, who can thwart him?" (Isa. 14:27).

Divinely Guaranteed

It is not a three-year outline of dated goals and action plans.

It is not a thirty-year road map to retirement.

Its goal is kingdom building for all eternity. Today's events are significant.

Significant for the Long Term

"My purpose will be established, and I will accomplish all My good pleasure" (Isaiah 46:10, NASB). There is no place, time, or person left out of God's plan. Every moment is nine months pregnant with his plan, awaiting delivery.

As East African missionaries with the International Mission Board, we have written plans—three-year plans, ten-year plans, and once a twenty-five year plan. We wrote plans for more years than could possibly fit into our actual years on the ground. I can write a plan as detailed as you want with a pithy vision statement, dates, actors, outcomes, incomes, entrance strategies, exit strategies, and so many sub-plots that you get dizzy. Then life happens. Eight military coups happened in those years—not one fit our plans. AIDS swept Uganda. Soldiers arrested missionaries, inconveniently. Unplanned inspired ideas resulted in digressions. Gas shortages put us in lines for whole days. Tires blew out so frequently that one pastor refused to ride with me anymore. Another serious plan-disrupter, the government communicated official decrees via radio. One radio announcement banned Baptist churches with immediate effect. Another airwave decree identified white men with beards as undercover CIA agents, so Jim made an unplanned dash home to shave. The proclamation that dropped two zeros off the local currency values messed with Jim the accountant's plans.

The beginning point and the ending point might resemble our plan, but nothing in-between looked like we thought it would. I smiled when I came across this tidbit from Eugene Peterson in *Take and Read*, "Goal-setting is, for the most part, bad spirituality."[3]

Don't get me wrong. I set goals and make lists, but I'm no longer emotionally invested in *my* plans. God has total veto power anytime he wishes to override my agenda. Sometimes I clearly discern what he wants of me, and sometimes I don't have a clue as to what he plans. One morning, after a peaceful quiet time including thoughtful contemplation as to the order of the day, a knock came at the door. The news bearer revealed that a young man, whom we trusted and had given lodging in our home, was a deceiver. The next step in *my* day's program would place our young daughter in potential danger, as I had planned an activity away, leaving her at home with a baby-sitter. I stepped outside a bit discombobulated. Looking into the vast African sky, full of bilious white clouds outlined with thick gold rims, the Spirit spoke to my spirit, saying, "Come on up and I want to show you gold, pure gold refined by the fire of myself." This spoke a calmness into my heart. It gave me confidence that though I was shocked, God was not. At least one line of this day's agenda had to do with my character and my walk with God. Adjustments changed my plan, and the first took my daughter to a friend's home for the morning.

We create our agendas. God has an agenda. Sometimes they coincide. Sometimes they don't. Our passions can harmonize us with God, or they can lead us down a discordant path. Sometimes we become confused as to the end goal. Our timing can be off. Still, we make plans. Always the question stands before us, whose plan takes priority, God's or mine? His plan is comprehensive, detailed, current-for-this-moment, divinely guaranteed, and significant for the long term. Frustration diminishes and profitability increases if I yield myself to his orchestration of the moment.

Our daughter Kristen returned to Virginia to attend Virginia Tech. April 16, 2007, the VT community experienced violent loss of life. Thirty-three students and teachers died, killed by a lone shooter. Desolation and despair abounded in the throes of a man's plan. Not one aspect of this event looked like God. Yet, we could trust ourselves to him in the midst of it, believing that even in this horror, God had something he wanted to accomplish, something within all of us experiencing this event. We did see compassion, love, community, and bold selflessness grow. Attitudes and priorities became more people-friendly. We saw kindness of character triumph. We found our hearts enlarged as we yielded ourselves to God within that horrid event. Certainly many events don't have the look of God's creative design. Other self-centric, evil, powerful influences work to shape the day. Through the most tangled mass of evil, God accomplishes his purpose, his plan, and desire. We have a choice daily. Do we allow the events of this day to cast us into despair? Or do we trust God to work toward his purposes in all circumstances? Read Romans 8:28. Can we allow that belief to shape our expectations, our responses?

During a college summer break, Kristen spent time in Afghanistan. Her schedule had a flight from Kabul to Herat. First attempt, the plane encountered bad weather and couldn't get over the mountains, so it returned. Second attempt, the pilot became ill en route, and he had no replacement, so once again the plane returned to Kabul. Third attempt, the flight reached its destination successfully. The passengers had options. They could expend energy-venting frustration over loss of time or the incompetence of the airline. They could allow fear to consume their thoughts, as they considered what might happen on the next flight. These options sprouted in the darkness of tunnel vision upon *man's* plan. A better option required a decision to enter into God's rest, to yield to God's plan, even if these passengers didn't have any idea as to what he might be doing. Often we cannot see his plan, and even when we do catch a glimpse, we may not understand. Nevertheless, we can reliably rest in God's agenda for the day regardless of the number of attempts necessary to cross those Afghan mountains.

Others have written well on God's purpose for our lives. I don't directly address God's purpose, the *what* and *why* of his plan, though it will surface often. I want to speak to the *how* of his plans. I work from the premise that God's plan, purpose, and desire flow toward fulfillment through his child's life in the ordinary moments of today. I offer practical suggestions to enhance that flow. First, let me tell another story or two.

God's Economy

Teaching Christians to pray gave me immense satisfaction and joy. After Kristen's birth, when I stayed at home more, I hosted a ladies' Bible study. We spent part of that time praying for friends who did not follow Christ. Diligently and persistently, we acted as priests on their behalf, by presenting their need to the Father. Wondrous answers followed. Another satisfying time, a few eclectic, hungry believers asked for further instruction in prayer. The book of Isaiah served as our text, as we prayed through its chapters. We met once a week for eighteen months and only finished the first twenty-seven chapters. The array of responses elicited and effects produced within our varied backgrounds startled and amazed me. That shared experience anchored my own life firmly in the Word. Prayer anchored in the Word proved efficiently effective, a wise stewardship of energy and time.

Later, Kampala Baptist Church where we were members selected a committee to advance the discipline of prayer among all members. Indeed these individuals prayed. But they needed greater maturity in prayer themselves before leading others to grow. Twenty to thirty members gathered once a month at our home for overnight prayers. (African committees worked on the village concept of consensus. Three or four people would never have been acceptable.) Travel after dark held risk and danger, so participants arrived directly from work and left the next morning. Before we gathered, each one prayed for his own life, confessing sins and leaving personal burdens with Jesus. This freed us to focus upon the people of God corporate, the larger body of Christ, and the awakening of our city to the good news of the Gospel. Those nights became glorious times of worship, singing, prayer, Scripture, confession on behalf of the church body, and intercession for revival and spiritual awakening. Our character and focus grew more like Christ's, and we melded into a community, eager to do the Lord's work.

During the late '70s and the early '80s, the disease AIDS arrived with nation-wide impact. At first, it didn't have a name. People, men and women, died from an unknown disease in which weight wasted away and infections proliferated. Witchdoctors came into their heyday, declaring it a curse and offering all sorts of costly cures. Desolation and despair fell upon people with AIDS. Treated as curses themselves, their families abandoned them to die alone, sometimes in a distant banana field. Deaths of young people soared. It reached critical mass, as it soon affected every aspect of society and life, including the church.

Within our local context, God had a specific plan. Not caught off guard, not slumbering from overwork, and not distracted by a crisis in another part of the world, God worked in this praying community. He had positioned that praying committee on the doorstep of its next assignment. These newly rejected, destitute people with AIDS needed to see—up close and personal—that God greatly loved them despite their condition. For two years, this *committee* had prayed for a visible, tangible, revelation of Christ's redemptive love within our city. God prepared us precisely to step into the AIDS event, to participate in the very answer we had sought. As a result, The Cup of Cold Water began and grew into a remarkable, well-known ministry of our church. The name came out of Matthew 10:42 where Christ urges his disciples to give "even a cup of cold water to one of these little ones" as an act of love to God. Caring for people with AIDS by sacrificially going, giving, and loving them to Christ, defined its mandate. Many believed God could and did want them, as they experienced the touch of Christians. Churches grew, adding worship services. The frequency of funerals increased also, becoming celebrations of the God who welcomed such a destitute rejected person into his kingdom.

Prayer for revival and spiritual awakening answered in the AIDS epidemic. Who would have thought? God works his plan, and it moves toward fulfillment through his people.

The church continued to grow. Repeated requests for prayer training came from more people than could fit in our house. The idea of a prayer seminar emerged as a gathering at the church building, overnight, one night a week for twelve weeks. These twelve nights of lessons trained us to pray for corporate revival for God's people and spiritual awakening for our communities. With vigorous preparation for lessons and logistics, excitement grew. But, I had a nagging problem.

A memory from three years earlier pushed its way into my thoughts. The remembered event involved taking my aunt to the grocery store back in Virginia. She had Parkinson's disease, which made her unsteady and sometimes a bit difficult to help. My turn to take her shopping came, so we went to the grocery store. She carefully selected her items and decided to splurge on a potted poinsettia. Eventually, we made our way through checkout, counted out the cash, and moved into the parking lot. I settled her into the passenger seat and then unloaded her purchases, placing the flower on the floor of the backseat last. Behind the flower sat a lone can of green beans. It hid from the cashier, as she rang up the flower without taking it out of the basket. What to do? Should I get my aunt out of the car and into the store again? I couldn't leave her alone in the parking lot to go inside and make the payment myself. I thought, "I'll take care of it later." And that was the last time I thought of it, until three years later.

That scene naggingly injected itself into my thoughts and then into my prayer. I rebuked Satan for trying to unsettle and distract me. I reasoned with myself that it couldn't be from the Spirit, since it happened so long ago, and how could I settle it now. I complained to God that I would become a laughable spectacle if I wrote the store and told them I needed to pay for a can of beans. My parents would be embarrassed, as our town was small and the sad tale would reach them eventually. This discussion took up more and more of the back-of-my-head space. The day before the first Prayer Seminar commenced, I drove the twenty minutes to the church for last minute arrangements. That back-of-the-head discussion nattered in full swing. A half mile from the church, reaching Wandegeya roundabout, a traffic circle, I said aloud, "Okay! Lord, we must settle this. What do I do? I will continue to circle this roundabout until this issue is settled." After only a few circles, I exited that traffic circle the same way I entered, and retraced the twenty-minute drive home. Writing the grocery manager, I told him simply that three years earlier I had stolen a can of green beans, and I included a check to cover the cost, plus interest. After a stop at the post office, I returned to the church. Settled!

Those overnight seminars were marvelous—exhausting but marvelous. The twelve-week sessions repeated many times. (When my daughter visited Kampala after her college graduation ten years later, she heard repeatedly how those seminars affected lives.) We held a church-wide overnight prayer after several cycles of these teachings. I boiled four hundred eggs to break the fast the next morning. Three hundred and eighty-nine people attended. Several made commitments to follow Christ during the night. I wondered in God's scheme of things, in his economy, how the one can of beans related to the four hundred eggs. His plan is comprehensive, detailed, and quite mysterious. Attention to the

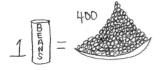

details of your day and a ready obedience in the small, even hidden, things can yield great profit.

All this fuss for a Bible!

Anthony arrived, a recent college graduate, who would work two years with our churches. We celebrated such arrivals for many reasons. New people usually asked the on-the-field people if they could bring an item for us from the US. Kristen needed a teen study Bible. A thief had stolen her former Bible from our locked vehicle while we ate lunch, one Sunday after church. Anthony brought her a nice one, full of extras, just right for a twelve year old.

A few—a very few—Sundays later, Kristen and I drove home from church in a small station wagon. As none of our vehicles had air-conditioning, we drove with the windows open. The new Bible in its frilly fabric cover lay on her lap. From the crowd on the sidewalk, a long arm darted through the window and grabbed her Bible. It didn't take but a few seconds for us to be hotter than that Sunday's equatorial heat. I started driving as fast as I could to follow him down the street, blowing my horn. He made a turn away from the road. I drove over the sidewalk and followed him down a footpath, still blowing the horn, dodging all sorts of people, animals, and objects, and squeezing between buildings. The small car maneuvered well, and we still had him in sight. Abruptly, a wide three-foot deep hole in the ground gaped in front of us, possibly the start of a building foundation. Halting immediately, Kristen flung the door open to continue on foot. Suddenly the troubling weight of my action pressed upon me. What had I started? I couldn't let her go alone. She didn't stop even though I started after her, calling her to come back. The car would disappear if I left it unlocked. It might disappear if I locked it. I returned to lock it. As I turned to resume the chase, a man intercepted me, right at my elbow, asking, "What's all this about?" "My daughter's Bible has been stolen from her lap," I hurriedly answered trying to continue after Kristen. His astounded retort came, "All this fuss is for a *Bible!*" That demeaning of God's Word raised my temperature a few more degrees, and I took off.

Kristen entered a narrow dark alley, disappearing from sight. I reached the alley entrance, in time to see her gather up her long skirt and jump

over a large steaming aluminum pot, atop a charcoal stove. The pot spanned the width of the alley. By the time I jumped the pot, she entered the light of a distant courtyard. Reaching the courtyard myself, I saw a man pull items out of the thatch covering the eave's rafters. He extracted several small bags, a radio, and a hat from the thatch, asking Kristen if any belonged to her. The folks in this courtyard looked surreal. All were men, very muscular. None wore a shirt, and a fine grayish dust thoroughly coated them—a puzzling sight indeed. Someone indicated that the thief took a left into the next alley, and Kristen moved on. I followed, leaving the wondering to another moment. About fifty feet into the next alley, she stopped, stooped, and scooped up her Bible. Apparently, the delay in the courtyard gave the thief his first chance to unzip the cover. Discovering *just* a Bible, he threw it to the ground and continued with the frilly cover.

Catching our breath, glad to be together, looking more closely at our surroundings, and hoping the car stood where we left it, we retraced our steps. The vehicle was there, surrounded by a press of people. I drove more cautiously back to the sidewalk, over it, and into the road. About then, the full weight of what I had done came to bear. Jim wasn't going to be happy with us, especially with me for taking unnecessary risks with our daughter in tow. Later we learned that those muscular guys, coated in gray dust, loaded bags of cement into railroad boxcars. This activity accounted for the coating of dust as well as their muscles.

Was this God's plan? I have my doubts, but I'm not certain. The longer I walk with him, the less confident I am of what he will or will not design into a day. Yet, I am confident that he was up to something in that event, something for good.

He Waits

You will seek me and find me when you seek me with all your heart.

Jeremiah 29:13

He does use angels, occasionally visibly. Angel Gabriel spoke with Mary (Luke 1:26).

He will use a donkey when he needs to do so. Numbers 22:21-35 has a good donkey story.

He will even cause rocks to cry out if we his people refuse to participate (Luke 19:40).

However, God prefers to use his people to implement his plan, to do his work. He desires that his children willingly offer their availability for his kingdom tasks. In truth, God will wait for this willing availability. God is patient not pushy.

Who are his people? His people are those who know that without God they can do nothing good (Romans 3:23, 7:18). God's people see themselves as redeemed, knowing that Christ has given them his righteousness, taking their sin upon himself (2 Corinthians 5:21). His people live confident that they are adequate in the Lord (Philippians 4:13, 19). God's people determine ahead of time to obey whatever assignment he gives, whatever the day brings (Luke 9:23, Colossians

3:17). God's people <u>pursue him with passion</u>—seek to hear, know, taste, see, touch, and enjoy him more fully each new day (Psalm 42:1). These are five characteristics, which define us as God's people. These same five characteristics make us available to him. God has called us and equipped us to labor with him in kingdom work.

Even so, erratic swings in mood, behavior, and priorities can play havoc with these characteristics. Some days, we move on the same page with God, and other days *clueless* better describes our walk. Yet, God still waits for us to participate in his agenda. He works patiently behind the scenes to bolster willingness and confidence. His Spirit steadfastly works to give us clean hearts and a hunger for God's ways. He does not become restless or impatient. Neither will he force his plans against our will. God waits! He restrains himself, waiting for us to say, "Yes, I am here. What is my task?"

Strengthening the last characteristic listed, the passionate pursuit of God, provides the essential impetus for consistent participation in his plan. The more I learn of God, the more wondrous he grows to me, and the more pervasively he inhabits my life, my thoughts, and my day. I begin to see him everywhere. The more clearly I grasp his nature and desire, the bigger he becomes and the taller he rises. As he grows bigger, I grow smaller. As he grows taller, in contrast, I grow shorter. In the presence of God's towering character and capacity, arrogance and self-absorption wither. Insisting on my plans, my way, or my suggestions becomes ludicrous. Humility increases, perspectives align with God's Word, and I become both pliable and wiser. John the Baptist said, "He must become greater; I must become less" (John 3:30). What nourishes a passionate pursuit for God? Every day ask God to make you hungry for him. Devour God's Word so that you know him. He's waiting.

God restrains himself, waiting, longing for us to step up to the plate. On day one, when I recognized my sin and my need, when I asked for forgiveness and yielded to his lordship, I began my journey with Christ into a transformed life. On that day, Christ removed my sin-stained clothing, wrapped me in his robe of righteousness, and placed his Spirit into me. Read 2 Corinthians 1:21-22 and 5:21, and Isaiah 61:10. From day one, God was ready to put me to work.

When in my twenties, I attended a foot washing service. A strikingly tall, older, distinguished seminary professor washed my feet. I remember the flood of emotions as he stooped way down to wet the cloth in the bowl and wipe my feet. The contrast overwhelmed me. It felt inappropriate, as if something was way off balance. The more I passionately pursue God, the more amazing our relationship becomes. He, the creator of the universe, desires to be my friend! He, the perfect One, wants to walk with me the far-from-perfect one. The better I know him, the taller God gets, and wonder increases. The taller God becomes in my sight, the easier it is to spot him above the clamoring demands of the day. That growing contrast increases wonder and humility. Both wonder and humility shape me to be available for his agenda. He waits.

Another *tall* experience occurred in arid northern Uganda during a ten-day team teaching event with several churches. We stayed in a mud-walled, grass-thatched house with no electricity and very little water, which came from a distant borehole. I bathed from a small bucket in the dark, behind the home. Drinking water required boiling to kill pathogens, so we drank hot tea. Cool drinks lived only in our dreams. This particular day, we walked several hours in the dusty heat of the African sun. At a pause in the journey, I plopped down prone on the ground in the shade of a large tree, so tired and so thirsty. Mike Bita, a fellow teacher and a tall man, stopped under the same tree. He stood towering above me. He towered over me when I stood beside him, so he really towered over me as I laid flat on the ground. With a broad grin, he leaned way down and handed me an orange, an amazingly unexpected, welcome gift. That event pictured God, so much larger than me, so willing to stoop down to reach me, and so happy to give good gifts. A passionate pursuit of God enables him to loom large over life, making him harder to miss and easier to trust. I spend less time and energy seeking help and satisfaction from other places. When he towers over me, he has my attention.

A passionate pursuit of God draws me deeper into his light. As his light increases, sin issues surface and are resolved. He works Christlikeness into my life. As he increasingly captivates me, the grip of self-absorption loosens. Christ-absorption replaces it. As I grow to think more like him, I recognize and accept his directions and provisions along the way. Pursuing God with passion *is* the path of discipleship. This pursuit not only emboldens us to step confidently into the right place but also prepares us to do the right thing. God's people must recognize themselves as sinners, redeemed and equipped by his Spirit. Available proactively for whatever he asks, they pursue him with passion.

Ugandan men and women infected with AIDS who have embraced Christ embodied these characteristics well. Full of disease, shunned, seen as cursed by evil spirits, and with no hope for a better future in this world, they knew that they're sinners in despicable conditions. I've heard many of them say, "The only good thing about me is Christ!" They loved Christ and pursued him with passion. They gathered on Saturdays at Kampala Baptist Church for praise and worship. Some days the disease had so weaken them that they couldn't sit upright. They laid on the unpadded wooden benches, with arms swaying in worship, singing, praying, and rejoicing in their redemption all day long. Whatever God asks, they did. "There is nothing else worth doing!" they responded. My faith stretched, gained muscle, as I witnessed their passion.

The prophet Zechariah in chapter 6:1-8 saw four chariots with massive muscular horses pulling, stamping, snorting, and eager to go, but they couldn't move ahead until the Lord said, "Go!" The all-powerful Sovereign, God, exercises patience. He waits to see his people pulling, stamping, snorting, and eager for the command "Go!" God waits for passionate people. "You will seek me and find me when you seek me with all your heart" (Jeremiah 29:13).

If I won't step up to the plate, I'll miss out. His plan will continue through another. Not one of us is indispensable. If I say no, he will ask someone else. But why would I do that, refuse his assignment? "There is nothing else worth doing!"

If you have trouble thinking that God can accomplish his plan using you, I suggest you review the stories of the Old Testament. Consider those whom God used to advance his story: Adam, Eve, Cain the murderer, Abel, Noah, the builders of the tower of Babel, Abraham, Sara who laughed at God, Hagar, Ishmael, Isaac, Esau, Jacob the deceiver, Leah, Rachel, Judah and his daughter-in-law Tamar, Joseph, Moses the poor speaker, Joshua, Rahab the prostitute, Samson, Deborah, Eli, Samuel, Saul, David the adulterer, Bathsheba, Solomon, Absalom the rebel, a whole host of ungodly kings, at least one Jezebel, and some very reluctant prophets. Also, consider the constant assault from evil nations, such as Assyria, Babylon, and Persia. If God can maintain his plan through those thousands of years with some weird curve balls thrown at him, he can use anyone whom he chooses. He has chosen you! He waits for you.

Sarah N.

Born in 1960, a member of the Basgoga tribe in eastern Uganda, Sarah grew up in a Muslim family. Despite Uganda's long history with Christianity, Islam increasingly claims allegiance. Uganda's Islamic neighbors to the north exert a steady pressure to make this happen. At age seventeen, Sarah had the first of five children, three by the first husband and two by the second. In 1990, after separation from the second husband, she discovered her HIV positive status and registered with The AIDS Support Organization, TASO, a non-government secular organization. Often Pastor Daudi preached at TASO gatherings, and after hearing him several times, Sarah decided to visit his church.

March 1991, Sarah recognized Christ as her Redeemer and decided to follow him. Three weeks later, she came to the pastor saying, "I have a big problem." Sarah shared her story, including her HIV infection and struggle with AIDS. Daudi explained the promises of Scripture, and the sufficiency of Christ in all circumstances. She eagerly sought to learn more and Pastor Daudi baptized her in May. Christ and the church moved to first priority in Sarah's life. She participated not only on Sundays but also in weekly fellowships, home cell groups, and outreaches into the community.

As she weakened, she came to stay with an aunt, a Muslim, who lived near the church building. The aunt told Sarah to sleep in the outdoor kitchen where three mud walls formed a five-by-seven foot enclosure around the charcoal stove. She slept on a straw mat facing the open fourth side, with a piece of plastic as a blanket. Twice, as she slept, thieves stole this plastic blanket. Sarah had two children with her, the youngest, three and a half years old. Her older child enrolled in the church's catch-up class for kids who had missed schooling. Sarah sold deep fried breads for income. Her health had the typical ups-and-downs of AIDS, some days strong and others weak. Shortly, her brother came to the same aunt, seeking accommodation. He too had AIDS. He slept in the same kitchen with Sarah.

The pastor and Patrick, a university student, had visited them and had seen their situation. They built a fourth wall and door onto the kitchen. Church members donated a mattress and blanket. As members continued to visit and to care for Sarah, the aunt became embarrassed and moved Sarah and her brother into the house. In the ensuing months, members continued to visit, taking food, sometimes helping her to walk back home from church, and assisting her to go to the clinic. This consistent and persistent demonstration of care eroded the Muslim hostility toward these Baptists.

Sarah matured in Christ, increasing in faith and hope and in commitment to her church family. She visited and cared for others. Patrick described her as clearly living one day at a time, not worried of death. She brought her brother to talk with Pastor Daudi, and her brother began to follow Christ. He in turn cared for Sarah through her last month of bedridden illness.

In September 1991, terribly ill with rashes, severe nausea, diarrhea, fever, and pain, Sarah died. When she died, the Muslim family rejected her body, saying she belonged to the Baptists. Church members bought a coffin and a burial place in the city cemetery. They brought food to her family, as they gathered for the traditional night of mourning.

As church members spent the night before the funeral with the family, the expected harassment from the Muslims never appeared. The preceding months of unexpected care quenched antagonism. Her funeral service, held at the church, took place the next day. Muslim African culture compelled the family to attend, but they refused to enter the sanctuary. They sat on the verandah circling the building. The P.A. system broadcast the service loud enough so that no one missed a word. The gentle, caring attitudes and actions toward the relatives broadcast even louder. No one missed that message either.

Some days later, Pastor Daudi entered a public transport mini-bus full of Muslims whom he did not know. Nor did they know him. The topic of discussion? The astonishing event when the Baptists cared for Sarah all the way through death. God manages the big picture, while we are obedient to do our small part, perhaps simply constructing a door.

God has a plan and he wants his people to play their assigned parts.

Another Bundibugyo Story

A few years after our eventful tie-rod journey, Harry and Jacques went to visit and preach in those same churches. They stayed in the typical mud and thatch homes rather than in a tent at the district office. Aware of deadly snakes in the rain forest, Harry feared spending the night on the floor in his sleeping bag. His anxiety didn't ease as he noticed evidences of witchcraft in the structure, bottles buried in the threshold and certain twigs hanging from the doorframe. As they attempted to sleep, a woman silently crept to their doorway, which had no door, poured liquid into the bottles and made eerie motions across the opening. Praying fervently for the protection of Christ, eventually Harry fell into a fitful sleep, only to awaken with a terrifying striking at his head. Gripped by the image of a venomous viper, he prayed this was a dream. Screaming and scrambling out of his bag, falling over Jacques, he realized a duck had waddled into the room and stood pecking at the stuffing in his bag.

If God can use a donkey, could he also use a duck? Of course, he can, but perhaps this duck was Satan's tool to knock Harry off balance. Or perhaps God wanted to expose the debilitation of fear and deepen peace. Perhaps it was both. We don't know. He's not telling. Faith grows.

Mystery and Minutia

As the heavens are higher than the earth, so are my ways higher than your ways

and my thoughts than your thoughts.

Isaiah 55:9

You have heard that the Devil is in the details, but actually, God is the creative Master of details. In addition to a profusion of details, he enjoys creating mystery. I don't speak here of *The Mystery* described in the first chapter of Colossians—God's wondrous plan to rescue sin-damaged people by his Son's death on the cross, and to repair them by allowing Christ to live within them. I ask you to consider another mystery, the faith-building mystery that the Lord weaves into our day—those confusions that make no sense, those moments that leave us wondering, and those unexpected twists in our path.

Why all the mystery?

First and most obvious, we have <u>finite minds, those of the created</u>. The minds within our sin-prone bodies are severely limited. They can't begin to match the mind of our Creator. My mind can't even match the mind of a Jeopardy contestant. And yet, God has given our redeemed minds the capacity to know the mind of Christ, as seen in 1 Corinthians 2:16. Often, though, our self-absorption so clogs our thoughts that we have few brain cells available to grasp the wonder of Christ. Even if we have totally died to self, until we receive our glorified body in heaven, we can see only a dim reflection of God and the intricacies of his plan. Read this in 1 Corinthians 13: 9-12. For now, we see a tiny fragment of the whole picture. "Yet these are but [a small part of His doings] the outskirts of His ways or the mere fringes of His force, the faintest whisper of His voice! Who dares contemplate or who can understand the thunders of His full, magnificent power?" (Job 26:14, AMP). Mysteries remain because we are not able to understand all that God does within our day.

Second, if there were no mystery, how would we <u>learn to walk by faith</u> rather than sight? Daily God arranges multiple opportunities to stretch our faith. Without them, we would still be immature babes drinking milk, carried by others or barely crawling.

Third, mystery <u>builds expectation, eagerness,</u> into our lives. It increases passion. Passion moves us toward whole-heartedness for the Lord and his activity. The opposite of passion is boredom, and boredom is a sign of spiritual deadness. "I'm bored," says I have shut the door on the Lord. Nothing equals a good mystery to keep the spiritual juices flowing.

Fourth, the mystery of our adventure with God <u>allows him to receive all the glory</u> and not me. Mystery prevents the boastful mindset, which says, "I knew that, I'm not surprised. It was my plan all along!" Mystery keeps us a bit off balance, so that we lean upon God rather than ourselves. He says, "I am the Lord; that is my name! I will not give my glory to another" (Isaiah 42:8). Mystery accomplishes that. It counterbalances our lust for recognition.

Fifth, <u>if we saw the whole picture, overwhelming inertia, or fear might result</u>. We might say, "No." We might say, "I can't," when God knows we can. He knows how much to reveal at what time. Trust him to do what is right. Live thankful that he hides much of the whole story from us.

God writes mystery into his plan for many reasons. Arrogance and foolishness lead me to demand that the Creator explain himself fully to me the creature. Consider Abraham saying to the Almighty, "I'm not moving until you give me a Google map laying out the details of the journey." We do know the direction of the journey, the joy that lies ahead, and the trustworthiness of the leader—sufficient knowledge to move us forward, despite the mystery.

Why the minutia, the myriad tiny details?

First, <u>God's creativity has no bounds</u>. He created all the stars, leads them forth every night, calls them by name, and by the greatness of his might and the strength of his power has not lost even one of them (Isaiah 40:26). His capacity for detail exceeds our wildest imagination. He enjoys his creativity. We should also enjoy it.

Second, <u>wonder will grow</u>. Have you watched a Discovery channel program as it displays layer after layer of incredible detail in the life of an obscure tiny insect? Does it not increase your sense of awe at the capacity of our Creator? Look at Zechariah 9:9 and 11:12. Compare them with Matthew 21:1-7 and 26:14-16. Look them up now; don't wait! What about those details? You are aware that four hundred plus years separate these two books, aren't you? Does your wonder grow? God continues to grow taller.

Third, <u>we all have a part to play</u>. Can you fathom writing a drama for a cast of millions? Every individual in the body of Christ has a part to play, written specifically for him—in fact a part written for this day, and another created for tomorrow. Such a drama requires an abundance of detail.

Fourth, tiny details format <u>God's training program</u>, his pathway of discipleship. We demonstrate faithfulness in little, then in much, as in the parable of the steward in Luke 16. The smallest assignments test the willingness of our heart, the tenacity of our passion, and the depth and purity of our obedience. Our response to the minutia presented daily may actually outweigh the importance of those big tasks he occasionally gives us. The big jobs stand upon a deep rock-solid foundation of tiny obediences, carefully and consistently laid, as bricks, each day. God, speaking to Joshua and Zerubbabel in Zechariah 4:10, instructs them to not despise the day of small things. One stone at a time and this huge task of rebuilding the temple and the city will reach completion. The rebuilding progresses as each plays his small part under God's leadership.

Fifth, minutia <u>keeps us humble</u>. Consider a multitude of tiny details forming a picture or story, which flows into eternity. No one piece overwhelms another. Every detail grows out of innumerable preceding details. My detail dovetails into so many others, just as a single strand of thread in a magnificent tapestry. One thread has no foundation for boasting. With these thousands of single threads, self-absorption finds it difficult to declare, "Look at me! See how great I am!" Zechariah tells us that we dare not despise the day of small things. One stone at a time and *God* will get the job done.

As with mystery, God has many reasons to love and use minutia. Sheer arrogance and utter foolishness lead us to demand that the Script Writer give me the actor a more substantial, flashier part. Consider Zechariah thinking, "Thirty pieces of silver is ridiculously low, I'll give the story more pizzazz and write in one hundred pieces." Little did he know that hundreds of years later *thirty* pieces of silver would appear in Judas' hand.

Mystery and minutia are indeed hallmarks of God's plan. He delights in creating them. Do you enjoy having a surprise for your friends? Do you enjoy it when they get into guessing what it is, anticipating the gift that you have chosen for them? Why shouldn't we delight in God's good gifts? Pray, asking for a spirit of eager, delightful anticipation, for this day's assignments from the Lord, the part he has written for you. God is pleased when we love the mystery of it all, when we walk in expectant faith, and when we give ourselves fully to every tiny detail he assigns. Wonder grows.

Sparrows are important

Darla, a lovely, energetic young woman, came to spend two years working with us in Uganda. Beyond understanding, early Palm Sunday morning, she died in her sleep. The *whys* go unanswered. That long, draining, and stressful Sunday was choked not only with grief and shock but also with the frustration of dealing with local police, immigration officials, and a woefully inadequate phone service. Late that night, I extravagantly filled the bath with hot water and soaked in bubbles up to my chin. I needed a quiet, private space and time to settle. Seven-year-old Kristen knocked on the door and asked to come in. She wanted to read a story to me from *Little Visits with God*. She discovered the day before that she could read this book for herself, reading eleven stories before she fell asleep Saturday night. The last story read, *God Counts Our Hairs*, filled her mind. This story she wanted to share with me. She read that the Father in heaven cares for the sparrows, and not one of them falls down dead unless he lets it fall. If God takes care of the sparrow, don't you think he can take care of you? Exactly what I needed to hear. What timing!

The Criminal Investigation Officer who worked on Darla's case came to her memorial service. What he saw surprised him. He had never attended a Christian funeral. He found plenty of sadness but not the wailing and mourning he expected. He heard in the whole service a message of hope and triumph. Afterwards, he asked many heart-felt questions and decided to adopt this way of life led by Jesus, as a superior way. The next Sunday, he brought his wife to the same Nakawa Church, and she made the same choice. They expressed amazement at finding a place of hope in their perpetually distressed Uganda.

We still do not fully comprehend the big picture of this event. We do know that God wove together the sacrificial life of a godly woman, the hardness of a criminal investigator, a wife without hope, a small church in an impoverished area, and even a child's new found eagerness for reading. His glory grew through this event, partly by drawing two people into his kingdom. No doubt, these were a small part of his doings, only a few of the strands he braided into that event.

Much to contemplate!

Okay!

Years earlier, walking home from a seminary class with the usual stack of heavy books, I felt impressed to visit Marie. I shrugged it off. Weary in mind and body and laden with books, I had a supper to prepare. Reaching our apartment, digging into my purse, I couldn't find my key. That locked door seemed to taunt me. "Okay! Okay! I'll go visit Marie." The walk was short. Marie, in tears, tentatively invited me to enter. She wrestled with a troubling issue, one that matched a struggle in my own life from a few years back. Amazed and rebuked, my spirit said, "Yes Lord, this is very much okay." Do you suppose God knew the stubbornness of my heart, the laziness of my body and the skewedness of my priorities, such that he hid my key? Would he do that for Marie?

On the Road

Some Ugandans identified driving as my spiritual gift. I spent much time in Africa moving people and goods from point A to point B. Uganda's population far outnumbered vehicles, even in our capital city. Whenever I opened the driver's door, a host of want-to-be passengers appeared. Sundays after church, our van filled with friends who lived along our route. One Sunday, dropping passengers all along the way, we neared home and realized Kristen wasn't with us. We had not detected her absence in the crush of riders. Back to church! Most of the time, I drove a small station wagon, so small that if you allowed too many kilograms of people to sit on the floor in the back, the front wheels no longer had traction on the road. I have had to stop and rearrange passengers to proceed. I have driving stories! Three wide-eyed goats staring at me, filling the rear-view

mirror is still memorable. Kristen sat in the backseat to keep them from leaping to the front. Another notable driving moment happened along Gaba Road on my way

into town with several passengers and already behind schedule. One lady standing on the roadside caught my eye. She motioned for me to stop. I did see her but decided, "Not today" and continued toward town. Sixty seconds later, God's Spirit said to my spirit, "I wanted you to give her a ride!" I turned around, went back, but she had gone. He laid out the mystery and the minutia for that moment, and I chose to ignore it. What had I missed? What had she missed?

Stop! Take a break! Find a jigsaw puzzle.

Work it as an act of worship and prayer.
The outline below will help.

Praise God

- for designing such an intricate kingdom.

- for fitting our many and varied shapes into oneness in Christ.

- for creating significance for each piece.

- for having a master plan, which he will achieve.

Forgive me

- for wanting to be a different shape. Teach me contentment.

- for demanding to see the whole picture, now. Increase my faith.

- for desiring to be a bigger piece. Train me in humility.

- for thinking that if I don't play my part, it won't be noticed.

Omit one puzzle piece. Meditate on that vacant spot

Help me Lord

- not to be a piece missing in action, muttering, "No big deal! What does it matter? Who cares? I'll not get involved. Don't pick me. I'm out of here. Choose someone else."

- to delight in the place you have designed for me.

- to consistently obey, to allow you to place me as you want.

Do whatever you need to do in my life, so I may fit your plan perfectly. Mold and prune me, so that I reveal your glory, your story, your picture.

The Oil Pipeline

Not by might nor by power, but by my Spirit, says the Lord Almighty.

Zechariah 4:6

Step into the imagination compartment of your brain. Visualize a solid gold lamp stand, the Jewish version, the one that occupied a prominent position in the temple. It has seven lamps branching from a single stem. Each lamp, shaped like a bowl, has seven spouts pinched into the rim. These spouts support wicks, which trail down into a central pool of oil. Seven flames burn around each of the seven lamps. Twice a day, priests enter the temple to trim the wicks and refill the oil.

Read the fifth vision in Zechariah 4:1-14.

Zechariah, a prophet, was familiar with the temple lamp stand. However, the lamp stand of this vision had anomalies, which caught his attention. First, two olive trees grew at the lamp's edge, one standing on either side. Second, an additional bowl hung above the seven sets of seven lights. The olive trees had golden pipes that channeled a continuous stream of oil into the higher bowl, which in turn continuously fed down into the bowls of the seven lamps. This new arrangement eliminated the necessity of refilling the oil twice daily.

Zechariah asked, "What are these, my Lord?" In essence the angel replied, "Don't you know what it is? Look again. Think about it." Zechariah re-examined the vision but still did not understand. He asked again, "What is this I see?" The angel responded, "Not by might, nor by power, but by my Spirit, says the Lord Almighty." He gave the underlying core meaning without any explanatory details.

After seventy years in Babylonian captivity, these Israelites faced an enormous challenge upon returning to Jerusalem. How could so few people—under equipped, over stressed, and besieged by persistent enemies— rebuild a city and the temple? This small band faced a mountain of rubble, piled from the Babylonian destruction of Jerusalem and compacted by the weathering of years. From where Zechariah stood, the task looked massive, a mighty mountain of work. Zerubbabel the city administrator and Joshua the priest surveyed the site with dismay. God sent this lamp stand vision to these two men to encourage them that they would indeed see this mountain of rubble conquered, and that shouts of rejoicing would accompany the task's completion. God, who started it, would complete it. Therefore, keep at it, one brick at a time, placing one stone upon another.

Don't believe the lie of the mocking enemy that the little things do not mount up to completion. Two enemies ridiculed the Jews as they worked to rebuild the walls of their city. Sanballat yelled out, "What are those feeble Jews doing? Will they restore their wall? Will they ever offer sacrifices in a temple again? Do they think that they can get everything back to normal overnight? Can they bring stones back to life from those burnt heaps of rubble?" Tobiah added his taunting. "What are they building? If a fox climbed up on it, he would break down their wall of stones!" The enemies of God's activity excel in mockery. When their taunts begin to discourage you, as you face your tasks, read of Sanballat and Tobiah in Nehemiah chapter 4.

This vision of the golden lamp assured these few Jews that not only would they complete the task but also they would finish it well. The plumb line in Zerubbable's hand gave evidence of a job accurately done. The two olive trees symbolized God's arrangement for a continuous flow of his Spirit through the two chosen leaders, enabling them for the task. God supplies sufficiently for the task that he assigns. Light represents life in abundance and God himself. God is strongly present (seven times seven) and his empowering oil, representing the Holy Spirit, flows freely. Do not despair.

From where we stand today, we may not see a mountain of rubble as Zerubbabel and Joshua did. Nevertheless, the underlying meaning of the vision holds true for us. Scripture contains layers of meaning for different peoples and times. We do face mountains of challenges. God provides the indwelling Holy Spirit, Christ in us, available continuously. God promises to finish that which he has started with us. We move forward one brick at a time. Shouts of rejoicing will accompany that day of completion when we step into perfection, measured by God's plumb line. The enemy still taunts. "You will never finish that task. You don't have what it takes. Who do you think you are? If even a fox climbs on your work, it will fall flat!" Do not listen to these lies. Jesus and the Holy Spirit continually pour themselves into us. The mountains we face will level. We do live in the kingdom of Light. God's presence is strong and his oil flows. Do not despair.

Don't take my word for this. Please test it for truth by reading these verses in the Word: Deuteronomy 31:6, John 16:5-15, Romans 8:26, Philippians 1:6 and 4:13, Colossians 1:13, 19-20, 27 and 2:2-3, and Hebrews 2:10-11, 7:25, and 13:5-8.

Speaking of the future Jerusalem, the city of God's people, the vision reveals, "I myself will be a wall of fire around it [his people], declares the Lord, I will be its [his people's] glory within" (Zechariah 2:5). "Christ in you, the hope of glory" (Colossians 1:27). God provides all the oil necessary to keep the lamps burning bright. His plumb line, the Word, and the guidance of the Holy Spirit, keep us on track. His Spirit provides everything needed for life in the kingdom of Light. The fiery light of his glory, the weightiness of his constant presence, shines through us.

Visualize yourself accompanied by two olive trees, one on the right and one on the left. Hold this image as you travel through your day. If you excel in the imagination department, visualize seven flames on your head. Ask God to anchor this truth in your soul, so that it provides practical and pervasive encouragement for your days.

Do you still find it difficult to believe? Contemplate these verses.

Philippians 1-4 and 2 Corinthians 5:5-9: Note Paul's God-confidence versus self-confidence.

Romans 5:1-11, 8:28-39: Dwell upon the often repeated "much more."

Ephesians 1 and 2: Make a list of the riches. Matthew 6:25-34, 7:7-11: Name the possibilities. Colossians 1 and 2: Explain the significance of Christ dwelling in me.

2 Corinthians 3:4-6, 4:6-7, 9:8: Define adequacy, and competence. Consider yourself a clay pot, even a cracked one, filled with the treasure of God's light shining through the cracks

"God will meet all your needs according to his glorious riches in Christ Jesus."

Philippians 4:19

Why do we doubt and resist?

Why do we substitute our own might and cleverness for the Spirit?

Do we prefer the twice-daily effort of refilling the oil as a better plan?

Ice Cream and an Umbrella

In June 1977, tensions rested heavy upon Uganda. Idi Amin's reign backed by Libya's Gaddafi moved into its sixth year, and his war against the prosperous and the educated continued. He had expelled Asian businessmen years earlier, and still prominent Ugandans disappeared with disturbing regularity. On June 19, screams from across our back fence ruptured our sleep. Vehicle tires screeched, and their doors and trunk lids slammed. Sounds of gunshots, heavy boots trampling, women screaming, the high pitched trilling of terror, and the African wail of mourning filled our neighborhood. The manager of yet another local industry disappeared that night, thrown into the trunk of a vehicle, never to reappear.

We had invited several friends to our home to churn ice cream that following afternoon. Our distressful night and churning anxiety made me want to cancel the event. But the goal of building relationships and the need for community overruled. The Italian wife of the steel plant manager, the Ugandan bookstore owner, the Dutch Catholic brother, the British girls' school headmistress and her boyfriend from Kampala all came. Neither preparations, pleasantries, the tropical beauty of our backyard, nor the cooling limbs of the sturdy mango tree over our patio eased the gnawing within my soul. The churning of the ice cream

finished, I sat with my bowl in this circle of friends and looked up into the shady bowers of the tree. Our mango tree was large, with long limbs. From underneath it appeared hollow as the leaves made a dense covering out on the tips of the branches. It looked as though we sat beneath a giant umbrella with thick ribs. At that moment, God clearly spoke, "Linda, it doesn't matter what rains down on the outside of the umbrella. I will keep you covered, so that you may live each moment within my peace." In that instant, the stress and distress drained away. My soul filled with peace beyond understanding, and his peace enabled me to give myself fully to our guests and God's activity in that time and that place. Being in God's will doesn't ensure safety, but it does always offer peace.

June 20, being my birthday, meant Baptist churches all across America had my name for prayer. A coincidence? No, rather, God provided exactly what I needed, when I needed it. He used his people's prayers to get the job done.

Oh what a clatter!

The kitchen was rarely dull in Uganda, even beyond the wonder as to whether this day might have electricity and water or not. Visualize the day I came in to find an appropriate technology volunteer using my kitchen as his lab. He concocted an organic pesticide in my blender and forgot to affix the lid. Smelly sticky green droplets rained down from the ceiling. Another eventful early morning, I went to start the coffee. A crinkling sound from under the microwave caught my attention. A snake slithered atop the recycled aluminum foil stored there.

A vivid memory lives of the evening we had invited Chinese diplomats to our home for dinner and to hear a small African a cappella choir. I made last minute preparations in the kitchen, fortunately behind a closed door.

A rat—I don't use the word *mouse* for a reason—ran into a lower cabinet through its open door. Panic! These were special guests. I didn't want to offend them. Ugandans would understand this situation but maybe not the Chinese. I grabbed the cat, threw him into the cabinet, closed and barricaded the door. Unfortunately, that cabinet housed baking pans, muffin tins, and cookie sheets. Such a clatter arose! But the cat succeeded. I tossed the cat with his rat out the back door. I found it difficult to walk back into the living room and not respond to the queries on our guests' faces. I did manage to give Jim the look, "Don't ask!"

Being in God's will isn't necessarily predicable...

But he does provide everything needed, even a handy cat.

The Process

Thus, you have my premise

God sets down an agenda for this day, giving us a part to play. He waits
patiently for us to do and be what he desires. He designs fruitfulness
into every moment. Though his agenda is full of mystery and minutia,
he provides everything required, as we step into his assignments. We
God's people can be in the right place, at the right time, doing the right
thing—consistently!

Sounds good? YES! But how do I get there?

I like to define The Process this way ...

- Come Hungry

- Delight in Being Chosen

- Catch Your Breath

- Hands Up!

- Leap Over the Fence

- Watch for Clues

- Listen and Hear

Come Hungry

O God, you are my God, earnestly I seek you; my soul thirsts for you,

my body longs for you, in a dry and weary land where there is no water.

Psalm 63:1

I'm embarrassed to admit how much food played into our thoughts in Africa. I packed four cans of cranberry sauce for the four Thanksgivings between furloughs to the States. I brought food coloring to make the white African sweet potatoes look American orange, and boxes of plain gelatin to make marshmallows to top those orange potatoes. We took canned hams, which didn't need refrigeration, for Christmas. Family tradition required four cans of blueberries for the first day of school muffins each year. Two or three jars of A1 sauce, grape jelly, apple butter, and sausage gravy hid in the back of the pantry for those infrequent times when we hosted only a few people around our dining table. It was a rare first night back in the USA that we didn't gorge ourselves on Fritos and French onion dip.

Actually, God didn't seem to mind such yearnings. As the first day of Kristen's seventh grade neared, I burrowed into my stash to get the last can of blueberries for this four-year-term. I failed to find any. I wracked my brain to think of a substitute for blueberries. It's amazing how desolate such a thing can make a mother feel. But God! A package, from my Aunt Elsie, mailed months earlier arrived the day before classes began. Another surprise, the customs officials hadn't ransacked the package as it moved through our post office. As you may already suspect, it contained a box of Jiffy Blueberry Muffin Mix. Another time, we hosted thirty-plus US short-term volunteers for a dinner, and I prepared beef barbeque for them. At the last moment, I realized my barbeque needed more sauce. What to do? I remembered the last bottle of AI sauce on the back shelf. Now really! These guys would be back in the States in a couple of weeks, and we were here for two more years. On the other hand, they had worked hard, and it was only food. In went the whole bottle. Those thirty arrived, filling our house. The last man through the door, the team logistics coordinator, handed me a bottle of AI sauce that one of the team members had brought from the US. As he handed it to me, he said, "I really don't know why this guy brought it, but perhaps you can use it." God must take great pleasure in delighting his children. I've chuckled over that bottle of A1 sauce many times.

These African tidbits don't fit a Sunday morning missionary testimony. However, they do represent the mystery and minutia within God's plan. He does enjoy his creative capacities.

Do you want to experience God in every day? Do you want to see him at work and hear his voice of instruction? Do you want to know him and his plans? Do you want to get in on the big picture? Then you have to *really* want it. You need a raging hunger in your soul for God. Your hunger for him must surpass all other hungers, certainly beyond A1 sauce or blueberry muffins.

You may ask, "How do I get to that place?" I suspect that a hunger already exists deep within your soul, but you've habitually suppressed it.

You've told yourself that you are not hungry, shushing those rumbles for something more. You've said, "I'm okay," and then gone forth to busy yourself with greater activity for the Lord. Busyness muffles that inner voice, which asks uncomfortable questions. Both habitual suppression and constant activity lead to an anemic, shriveled hunger. Allow me to tell you of four steps that you can take to awaken and strengthen your hunger for God.

First, give voice to the gnawing dissatisfaction in your soul. Admit aloud that you are sick and tired of barrenness in your walk with Christ. Share with a friend your weariness with the *same ole same ole* monotony of endless doing without an inner energizing passion. The Spirit fuels passion for God. In prayer ask the Lord probing questions and listen for answers. "Is this discontent from you? Why don't I have a hunger for you? How, when, and why do I stifle the inner rumblings for more of you? God, what can you and I do about it?" This spiritual cancer of barrenness calls for far more attention than the physical cancers, which consume us. Discuss it with a friend. Examine it. Test it with Scripture. Try a day of fasting to sharpen your ears for listening and to sharpen your hunger for God. Thank God for an opportunity to focus, to ask the hard questions, and to seek him anew. As an anonymous 14th century monk speaks of God in *The Cloud of Unknowing*, "With his great grace he kindled your desire and fastened to it a leash of longing and with this he led you"[4] to himself. Ask God to stoke the flame of desire and to tug on the leash of longing.

Next, cultivate a hunger for fruit. Read biographies of faithful, fruitful people. Start with Dwight L. Moody. Away from home one evening, he hired a horse drawn taxi to take him to a friend's home, where he would spend the night. As he paid the fare, Moody said to the driver, "Good night. I hope to meet you in glory." At midnight, that same driver awoke the whole house with his pounding on the door. Moody, opening the door, saw tears streaming down his face. The driver said, "If I meet you in glory, I have got to turn around. I have come to ask you to pray with me." Moody may not have been aware at the time, but he had moved on the same page with God when he spoke to that driver earlier in the evening.

Read of the great revivals of the past. Watch the movie *Amazing Grace.* Ask God to give you a passion for your assignment, as he gave Wilberforce for his assignment to battle slavery. Other life stories will fuel your hunger. God's people are passionate for him. Paul feared the Corinthians had lost their passion when he wrote that their minds had been "led astray from the simplicity and purity of devotion to Christ" (2 Corinthians 11:3, NASB). King David is described as a man after God's own heart, not because he was especially holy, or intelligent, or from a good bloodline but because he hungered after God. Two of David's Psalms form the next step to whet your appetite.

Pray <u>Psalm 27 in the mornings and Psalm 63 in the evenings</u>. Turn the lines of these verses into conversation with the Lord. "Lord when trouble looms, strengthen my confidence in you as my stronghold. May I see more of your beauty so that my eyes don't wander into other places." Choose one word or phrase from the verses to meditate upon through the day and another as you fall asleep in your bed. Print your favorite line on little papers and stick them on the cabinet door, the mirror, car dashboard, tube of hand cream, and the ice cube dispenser. This technique increased our Luganda and Swahili vocabulary. Meditation on the Word with visual reminders and repetition will captivate the thoughts in your head, and lead you into a growing hunger and thirst for the Lord. Work at this exercise until your passion matches the passion David expresses in these two Psalms. Apply Philippians 2:12-13 to this venture. Did you read it just now? Does the central phrase describe your pursuit? Cultivating a passionate hunger for God is serious business. Throughout the day, pray silently or aloud, "Lord Jesus Christ Son of God, have mercy on me." Watch his mercy create hunger and passion in your life.

Now, rediscover your imagination. God gave it to us. God molded us into his image at creation, and that God-designed image includes imagination. Imagination is one part of our makeup, which resembles God. Think about this. Is not God the most imaginative being in existence? Too often, we discard it as a childish thing. Pick it up again and give it to the Lord for dusting off and reactivating. Apply it to Scripture. Read Isaiah 40:12 and dwell upon the description of God as he measured the waters of the earth in the hollow of his hand. With your imagination, pick up the Pacific Ocean and put it in his hand. Add the Atlantic, Lake Huron, the Amazon River, Victoria Falls, and the creek in your neighborhood. See if you can reach his hand's limit and cause it to spill over. Read Matthew 14:22-32. Enter into this event. Would you have seen a ghost? Imagine yourself as Peter, when Jesus asks you to step out of the boat. Imagine yourself as Jesus, coaxing Peter to get out of the boat and step onto the water. Spend time with these images. Imagination requires unhurried, uninterrupted time, which is another reason why we often discard it as an adult. Imagine yourself among the seventy disciples sent out by Christ into the surrounding villages. Contemplate Christ as he washes your feet, and as he talks of the pearl of great price. Pretend you are Steven Spielberg making a blockbuster film from Revelation 8:1-5. Develop it with all the special effects your imagination can muster. Give some time to this exercise. You'll be surprised at what God can do, at what he will say, as you sit and dwell on his Word.

Imagine Christ appears to you in bodily form and says that he has three days, Friday, Saturday, and Sunday to spend in your community. He asks you to accompany him as he moves through your streets, into the mall, to a football game… Imagine an angel appears to you, and says, "I have an assignment for you today. God has used your past experiences to prepare you to _____." Does your imagined scenario seem any stranger than when Gabriel told Mary that she will have a child, and his name will be Jesus?

Let me give a warning. Imagination is susceptible to corruption by our own evil nature and by Satan. We must not live in the realm of imagination. But fully yielded to the Spirit, it serves as a useful tool for uncovering systematically suppressed desire for God, for awakening God-given hunger for him. Keep it attached to the Word and prayer. Sharing your journey with a fellow God-pursuer will safeguard you further.

Can you feel the hunger growing? Do you notice a hunger for usefulness and a disdain for futility? Has your soul expanded its hunger for deliverance from self-absorption and sin? Do you hunger to step into his assignments? Do you sense a building eagerness to get into kingdom work, advancing Christ in yourself, your workplace, and the world? Do you long to *be in on the know,* rather than wandering around clueless?

Following the overthrow of Idi Amin in 1979 and the stressful ensuing string of military coups, our director gave us permission to spend Christmas in the US. Normally, we returned to the States every fifth year, so we weren't due such travel for another year. Plans fell in place quickly. My eighty-six year old grandfather lived near the airport, thirty miles from my parents' home. We asked him to meet us at the airport, and drive us the thirty miles to my parents. We also implored him not to tell anyone of our plans. He was thrilled! "It has been years since I knew something before everyone else. It's invigorating to be in on the know!"

He spoke truth. Keep stoking that hunger. Feed the desire. Give it room to express itself. Allow desire the space to do something. As it grows, watch it purify and simplify, becoming a reaching out for God simply for himself. The 14th century monk mentioned earlier also said, "Knit yourself to him by love and by faith. And in virtue of that knot you shall be a regular partner with him."[5]

Knit yourself to him by love and by faith.

In virtue of that knot you shall be a regular partner with him.

A White Chicken

Nakku, a thirteen-year-old girl, was the first to follow Christ in her family. She longed to demonstrate to them the superiority of Christ over their traditional religion's fear and worship of ancestral spirits. Being only a young girl, she had little influence and certainly no money. As Easter approached, she continued to pray for such an opportunity. Though her family did not understand the truth of Easter, the extended family would come together for a big meal as a cultural celebration. Nakku asked God to give her something to take to that gathering to show his goodness. Walking to church early Easter morning, she passed through a commercial section of the city, and circled a large roundabout bordered by a school, a small hotel, and numerous shops. Off to one side, she spotted a large white chicken in the bushes. Going closer for a better look, she recognized that chicken as a freshly slaughtered sacrifice of witchcraft, probably attempting to nullify a curse. This place did hold spiritual significance for her clan with frequent witchcraft events in the past, before the city expanded into this area. It still held ancestral significance, but urban development made it difficult to access for religious rites. Her first impulse pushed her to walk away quickly. As she did so, it occurred to her that perhaps God had prepared a big white chicken for her family's Easter dinner. Turning around, looking to see if anyone involved stood in sight, she returned to the chicken. Convinced that her new Lord Jesus's authority overruled every other god's domain, she picked up the bird—right out from under the enemy's nose! Elation grew every step of the way, as she continued to church. The chicken lay under her bench during the singing and worship. Testimony time came, and Nakku stood quickly to go forward. She told the congregation of her desire for her family to know Christ. Then she narrated every detail of the story of her journey to church that morning, making much of God's goodness. At that point, she hoisted the plump white chicken over her head for everyone to see saying, "Glory to God! He loves me so much." The majority of the congregation at least inwardly gasped as she told her tale. Fear of witchcraft and those ancestral spirits would have prevented many from receiving such a gift from God. This young girl's confident faith in her Lord challenged everyone there. This thirteen-year-old girl preached the first sermon of the day. I'm disappointed to say that I don't know the rest of the story, but I would've loved to see the family's reaction. Most likely, that event of partnership with God still ricochets for his glory.

Mr. Okwii

A dignified, tall, thin, gray-haired man in a well-worn suit walked into Bible Way Correspondence School office. He asked for Linda Rice. He knew my name because I signed his course certificates. He introduced himself as Okwii, from a village in Teso, a northern district of Uganda. Our office was in southern Uganda. We sat, and he told me his story.

About two years earlier, he enrolled in Bible Way courses. God opened his mind to understand the Bible, and he came to realize that Jesus was actually God. He also came to see himself, Mr. Okwii, as a sinner who needed a forgiving Savior. At this late stage of his life, Mr. Okwii made a radical U-turn. With great earnestness, he told me that he wanted to live the rest of his days pleasing God. But he had a dilemma. He needed instruction. So he traveled two days on foot and on public transportation to reach the Bible Way office to talk with the director of his Bible courses. His dilemma—he had two wives. They had been his wives for more than fifty years, and he loved both of them deeply. Did God want him to get rid of one of them? If so, how could he choose which to send away? If he sent one away, who would care for her and where would she stay? No one would take in such an elderly woman. They could not make a living, as neither could read and their physical strength was long gone. He had no other land on which to build one of them a separate house. He had taught them the Bible Way courses and they believed in Christ. His emotions struggled, torn between his love for God and his love for his two wives. The intensity of his desire to please God, the lengthy and costly travel, and his consideration of such painful possibilities, moved me deeply. I told him that God blessed me, as I listened to his story. Indeed his wives were two richly blessed ladies to be so loved by their husband who had led them into God's kingdom. I assured him that God wasn't in the business of breaking up marriages. "Go home, continue to love God with all your heart, and he will enable you to care wonderfully for these wives. The Bible does say that you cannot be a pastor if you have multiple wives. Though you will not pastor a church, God does command you to teach others what you know of Christ as you live the rest of your years." Mr. Okwii, visibly relieved, thanked me over and over again. My love for the Lord grew that day because I saw his love in Mr.

Okwii, a humble precious man—a man hungry for God and passionate to please him. What a wondrous afternoon when God got taller and I got smaller. What a privilege when God assigned me a part to play in his work in that Teso homestead.

Delight in Being Chosen

You did not choose me, but I chose you.

John 15:16

Think back to your early years of school. Visualize a beautiful day, with your classmates outside, awaiting the commencement of the games. The teacher appoints two captains and instructs them to select teams, each in turn choosing a player. For some of you, pleasure already flows through your memory cells. You remember your names, called out first. For others of us, the thought evokes long ago dread. Please don't let me be chosen last!

What happens to us when we're chosen not for third place, not for second place, but we hear our name called for first place? How do we respond when the person of our dreams notices us, engages us in friendship, and opts for our company over others? What shifts in our psyche take place when a coveted award or a long-desired promotion comes our way? What does praise and recognition do for a child's self-esteem?

The King of Kings and Lord of Lords calls you, by name. Graciously and extravagantly, he chooses you, calling, "Follow me." He has ninety-nine sheep already in his fold, but he comes after you. He says "I have called you by name; you are Mine! . . . Since you are precious in My sight, since you are honored and I love you." (Isaiah 43:1, 4, NASB).

The prophet Zechariah received eight marvelous visions from the Lord, but the fourth one is my favorite. Turn in his book to chapter 3 and read verses 1-7. Now activate your imagination once again, and put yourself in the place of Joshua, the priest. Christ has made us into a kingdom of priests, as we see in I Peter 2:9. Joshua stands before two men. Satan, on his right, argues with the Angel of the Lord, whom we understand as Christ. Satan accuses as a prosecutor. "This useless guy, Joshua will disappoint you. He has a long history of sin. Look at his miserable appearance. Forget him!" But the Lord takes none of this nonsense, declaring, "Silence! I myself have chosen him. Is not this man Joshua a burning stick, which I myself have snatched from the fire?" Now admittedly Joshua, dressed in filthy rags, appears to fit Satan's description. These filthy rags do represent his long history of sin. But then to Satan's dismay, the Lord removes the filthy rags and dresses Joshua—you—in rich garments. "He has clothed me with garments of salvation, He has wrapped me with a robe of righteousness" (Isaiah 61:10, NASB). "God made him who had no sin to be sin for us, so that in him we might become the righteousness of God," (2 Corinthians 5:21). Satan had no more to say. The Lord won the case. Joshua, chosen by God himself, gained free access into God's house, his rule, and his plan. Jesus says, "You did not choose me, but I chose you and appointed you to go and bear fruit" (John 15:16).

God chooses us. Delight in it. A school playground choosing fades in the light of God's choosing. God chooses us to have a part in his grand plan that flows into eternity. We must delight in being chosen if we hope to partner with God. The vigor of our relationship with God and the quality of our partnership with him flow from this delight.

If Delight in Being Chosen weakens, I wander into a flurry of activity, trying to prove myself worthy. Futility, burnout, and dissatisfaction result. If I don't have a vigorous Delight in Being Chosen, then of necessity, I push the hunger for God into the far back country of my heart. I try to convince myself that satisfaction isn't possible. I begin to eat discarded cornhusks meant for pigs, attempting to satisfy myself with junk. Read the story of the prodigal son in Luke 15:11-31, and look for parallels. Delight in Being Chosen defines my hunger as a hunger for God, not as a hunger for activity, recognition, riches, or the love of others, and on and on.

This delight shapes my hunger for God into an eager anticipation of satisfaction, an expectancy of abundant fruitfulness. But with it comes restraint, a willingness to wait upon the Chooser to set the course. I'm able to delight in him without yielding to the compulsion to do anything until he says, "Go." Zechariah 6:7 portrays this truth with horses. The powerful, straining horses, eager for the run, waited until God said, "Go." Such a delight will produce both vigorous eagerness and the powerful restraint necessary to wait for God's instruction.

God has chosen us to enter into salvation, to wear Christ's robes of righteousness, and to live in partnership with him as kingdom builders. Too often, we don't believe this truth, opting for Satan's accusing lies instead. How often do we hear Satan's accusations? "You're worthless. Sin still entangles you. You can't do that. Failure is certain. Why would anyone trust you? Now look at what you have done! Who do you think you are anyway?"

Delight in Being Chosen deals a deathblow to self-absorption with our own unworthiness. We do need to live from a position of humility, and a portion of humility does come as awareness of personal sin and frailty grows. But by far, the greater portion of humility emerges in the process of drawing near to God. As he gets taller, we get smaller. Christ did not humble himself by digging about in past sins, since he had no sin. He humbled himself by accepting a position underneath the authority of God. Read Philippians 2:5-8. God made the decision to choose us despite our unworthiness. On the opposite end of the self-absorption spectrum, this Delight in Being Chosen also deals with arrogance and conceit, absorption with our goodness. Remember *Who* did the choosing. Christ's choosing of me has nothing to do with my goodness, or worthiness. On our own, we're utterly wicked, deceitful, and all our righteous acts are as filthy rags (Isaiah 64:6). Nevertheless, God chooses us. We can boast only in Christ. We do delight in his choosing. God says, "I have engraved you on the palms of my hands" (Isaiah 49:16).

Often traveling for Bible Way School, we'd stop at a school along our route and ask the headmaster to allow us to speak to the students. The school director sent a runner to tell the classes to gather. (You can tell I'm not talking about America!) I carried a large nail in my bag for these occasions. Looking around, I pointed out names scratched with some sharp point into the wooden benches and desks. Then I read the Isaiah verse, "I have engraved you on the palms of my hands." Ugandans were accustomed to writing notes, phone numbers, and names on their hands and arms with a pen because paper was scarce. I described how Jesus etched our names on his palms, not with ink but with the nails of the cross. When the nails of crucifixion pierced his hands, my name appeared on his palm. Yours did too.

He has chosen us. Delight in it! As believers, we respond to that choosing by embracing Christ's work on the cross, and by placing ourselves under his authority. This wonder and delight can diminish if we lose sight of our origins, if we are not careful and alert for distractions, and if we listen to Satan's accusation. Diminished Delight in Being Chosen yields stunted disciples. Guard against this by returning, again and again, to the story of the cross by reading and sharing this wonder with others. Participate often in the Lord's Supper, corporate worship, and meditation on the Word. Celebrate Easter each new morning, and declare every Sunday a resurrection Sunday. Cultivate the wonder of his choosing and delight in it. We don't have to be stunted disciples.

As Os Guiness says, we can "Rise to become the magnificent creatures only one Caller [Chooser] can call us to be."[6] (Brackets are my insertion.) Zechariah, in the middle of chapter two, says God considers us the "apple of his eye." Now would be a good time to read that whole chapter and revel in God's relationship with his Chosen. David writes a passionate psalm in which he relishes the wonder of being chosen. Read Psalm 18 in *The Message*. If you don't have a copy, find it on the internet at *biblegateway.com*. Read it aloud with passion.

He has chosen you! Delight in it!

Buy the prettiest apples you can find.

Eat one as an act of worship and praise.

Give away the rest, telling the recipients, "You are the apple of God's eye."

The Flower

Kampala Baptist Church, as part of their worship service, invite those with prayer needs to come forward. Ten to fifteen people might come. Then others from the church body step forward and take them outside the building to pray. One Sunday I stood at the back of the room, holding a fidgety, quite young Kristen. The pastor said, "We need one more person to come pray." Unusual! No one moved. I couldn't see the front of the church, as everyone else stood, also. I handed off Kristen to an usher and went to the front of the sanctuary. There stood a smallish man, whom I had never seen, standing military erect, looking sternly serious, and holding before him a small lovely red flower. Ah ha, this explains why no one came—an unknown quantity. I reached out to him. He took my hand and we went outside. Sitting down on the curb around the courtyard, I asked him to describe his prayer need. "God has asked me to do something great for him, and I am so unworthy. Pray that he will make me able to do this great thing." He spoke too loudly, too dramatically, and filled with emotion. Well, I can pray. So I prayed up one side of him and down the other, covering all the bases. I asked God to expose sin within him and to help him repent. To purify his motives. To clarify the details of the task. To banish fear. To humble every shred of pride. He prayed fervently with me throughout: "O yes, Lord. Do it, Lord. Answer as she has asked. Help me, Lord Jesus." After about fifteen minutes, we went back inside, he returned to the front row, and I circled to the back to retrieve Kristen. I had not asked his name or his task, nor did I tell him my name. The pastor led us in the Lord's Supper about two hours later. Though still at the back of the church, I could see the front, since the congregation now sat. As the drink and bread moved through the rows, this smallish man walked up on the platform, again seriously erect. This time he held out with both hands an extraordinarily beautiful long stem of brilliant red blossoms. He knelt below the large wooden cross on the wall. He bowed low with his face on the floor and the red flower extended as an offering. No one stopped him. Everyone saw him. No one knew him. (If this happened in Virginia, a couple of ushers would have led him away.) The pastor finished the supper, and the man returned to his seat. Worship songs and testimonies concluded the service. People didn't leave quickly. They stayed to fellowship for another hour or more. I stood in a chatting huddle, when a hand reached in and touched my elbow. A parting opened, and this smallish man said, "Linda Rice, today the Lord is pleased with what you have done for me." He walked out and we never saw him again. I do believe God chose him for that act of worship. Perhaps God gave him the assignment to model devotion before us that Sunday. Perhaps the beauty and simplicity of his act caused us to examine our own purity of devotion to Christ. Perhaps he was a man greatly forgiven, who asked for a way to show gratitude, and God gave him this opportunity. Perhaps God chose him to stretch my discipleship with a training exercise in not judging a man by his outward appearance. It may have been a test of obedience. I can only wonder and delight.

Catch Your Breath

Be still before the Lord, all mankind, because he has roused himself from his holy.

Zechariah 2:13

Bilbo Baggins, of J.R.R. Tolkien's *The Hobbit*, finds himself caught up in a previously unimaginable mission. He, a mere hobbit, naturally short and timid, must spy out the den of the dragon Smaug, an enormous, fire-breathing, vile creature. After a lengthy and mind-boggling trek, he comes to the portal of the dragon's lair. Immediately upon stepping inside, Smaug is no longer a nightmarish figment of his imagination. This living, breathing, mountain of legs, scales, nostrils, talons, and wings supplants the image with an undeniable hulk of reality. Even though Smaug sleeps, Bilbo feels immobilized, as if he has fallen from a high tree and had the wind knocked out of his chest. He can barely breathe. Smaug, surrounded by treasures—gold coins, goblets, jewels, and chests stacked ever so precariously—seems unapproachable. Bilbo moves cautiously around the sleeping beast, for he must find a flaw in his armor. His toe catches a golden goblet, and its metallic clank sounds like a death knell. Bilbo catches his breath, flattens himself against the wall, expecting the sleeping Smaug to arouse.

Consider these verses. I have inserted [catch your breath] to emphasize that far more than simply not talking is indicated. Read them thoughtfully. Put yourself into the setting.

> "Be silent [catch your breath] all flesh, before the Lord; for He is aroused from His holy habitation." "Quiet, everyone! Shh! Silence before God. Something's afoot in his holy house. He's on the move!"
> – Zechariah 2:13, NASB and MSG

> "The Lord is in His holy temple; let all the earth hush and keep silence before Him." "Oh! God is in his holy Temple! Quiet everyone—a holy silence. Listen!" – Habakkuk 2:20, AMP and MSG

> "Hush! [Catch your breath!] Be silent before the Lord God." "Quiet now! Reverent silence before me, God, the Master!"
> – Zephaniah 1:7, AMP and MSG

About now, I usually hear some version of these statements. Come on Linda, you push the point to the extreme? Such a breathless expectation sounds so Old Testament, but we have a greater knowledge of God than they did. Jesus came as a human like us. Such drama overdoes it these days. It doesn't fit. Get real.

But, I ask, does a greater breath-taker exist than the holy, creator, almighty, sovereign, all-knowing, ever-present, and awesome God, who moves himself and his plan through the moments of this day? Does it, at least, give you pause that this God restrains his all-powerful self, waiting for his people, you and me, to take up our assignments? Why doesn't this truth arrest our attention? We easily forget that the invisible kingdom of God is the greater reality, more authentic, more durable than the visible kingdom, which presses upon us. Much of what makes us breathless these days are vaporous shadows springing from our fears and lusts or an ad agency. They will pass away in the twinkling of an eye when God bursts out of the invisible realm, once again, into the visible. Perhaps the well-respected Oswald Chambers' thoughts on Catch Your Breath will carry more weight than mine do. Read this excerpt from "The Graciousness of Uncertainty" a devotional from *My Utmost for His Highest*.

Naturally, we are inclined to be so mathematical and calculating that we look upon uncertainty as a bad thing. We imagine that we have to reach some end, but that is not the nature of spiritual life. The nature of spiritual life is that we are certain in our uncertainty. . . . To be certain of God means that we are uncertain in all our ways, we do not know what a day may bring forth. This is generally said with a sigh of sadness, it should be rather an expression of *breathless expectation*. We are uncertain of the next step, but we are certain of God. Immediately we abandon to God, and do the duty that lies nearest, He packs our life with surprises all the time. . . . We are not uncertain of God, but uncertain of what He is going to do next . . . When we are rightly related to God, life is full of spontaneous, joyful uncertainty and expectancy. 'Trust also in me," said Jesus, not—"Believe certain things about Me." Leave the whole thing to Him, it is gloriously uncertain how He will come in, but He will come.[7] (emphasis mine)

<u>Anticipating something unexpected and unknown</u> can cause us to catch our breath. There are other reasons to catch your breath. Speaking of Aslan the Lion of Narnia, Mr. Beaver told Lucy, "He is good but he is not tame." Os Guinness quotes Oswald Chambers: "There is an aspect of Jesus that chills the heart of a disciple to the core and makes the whole spiritual life gasp for breath."[8] He refers to Christ as he set his face toward

Jerusalem like flint, and those who followed him were afraid as described in Mark 10:32-34. <u>Following our Lord can be dangerous and it certainly is serious.</u> "Our God is a consuming fire" (Hebrews 12:29).

O. Hallesby in *Under His Wings*, probing the phrase "work out your salvation with fear and trembling" in Philippians 2:12, wrote, "No man can escape feeling that there is something dangerous about God, provided he comes close enough to Him . . . The dangerous aspect of God was connected with His holiness, that is, His hatred of sin."[9] God is <u>unrelentingly serious against sin.</u> As he hands out assignments, he will purify us. "It is a dreadful thing to fall into the hands of the living God" (Hebrews 10:31).

"As the Father has sent me, I am sending you" (John 20:21). If you need to refresh your memory as to how the Father sent Jesus into the world, read again Philippians 2:5-8. Do you remember the opening of Mission Impossible TV episodes? A tape recording defining the mission, collected in some obscure spot, always began, "Your assignment, should you decide to accept it, is . . ." At the end of the recording, the tape self-destructed. This dramatic opening signified the enormity of the task. Our assignments from the Lord, should we decide to accept them, could require great sacrifice on our part, a giving up of rights, and even obedience unto death. <u>Anticipation</u> and <u>potential danger or sacrifice</u> are reasons to catch your breath before proceeding.

<u>Significance</u> is another. The awesome significance and power of *Who* gives the assignment causes us to pause. The enormity of his grace in that he chooses to give the assignment to *me* startles. Both are breathtaking. The possibility of misusing such grace can cause me to hesitate and tremble. The eternal reach of his assignments catches my breath with awe. Not

one of his desires, his wishes, or his plans is insignificant, of little value. If God asks me to take a cup of cold water to my neighbor, he weaves eternity into the request. Read Matthew 10:42.

If the above are not reasons enough for you to catch your breath, then I give you one more, a more pragmatic reason. Please do this: Stand up straight with shoulders back. Take in a deep breath and hold it there, filling your lungs with expectancy, anticipation, and fear with excitement. Put yourself on full alert. Now take note, <u>you are not talking</u>. In fact, you are unable to speak at this point, which is my point. Taking such a breath enables us to listen. This chapter's opening verses say, "Quiet! Hush! Shh! Be still! Silence! Listen!" We say that we want to be in the right place, doing the right thing, at the right time, participating in God's agenda. Even if we come ravenously hungry for him and filled with delight in being chosen by him, it yields nothing, if we will not catch our breath. We must give God our full attention, intentionally listening to know what he wants of us.

Silence! Catch your breath, everyone, before the Lord;

God is on the move in our midst.

Catch Your Breath moments of an entirely different type

As we drove down a footpath through elephant grass taller than our vehicle, their green tips touched across the roof of the van. A snake fell off the grass through the open window into the vehicle. Everyone, including the driver, jumped out. The van stopped a few yards away. Another day, on another footpath, such a huge Gaboon Viper crossed the van's path that in a fear response I slammed on the brakes, discombobulating us all. I allowed it to pass unharmed. The villagers would have preferred otherwise.

———

Jim and I trekked two hours through impenetrable rain forest on the steep sides of the Rwandan Virungu volcanoes. Often, we fell several feet through the tangled mass of undergrowth. Our feet seldom touched solid ground. After three weary hot hours, a large male silverback gorilla jumped out of the brush directly in front of us. Literally thumping his chest and screaming, he convinced us we weren't to come any closer. Our guide told us to squat down and act submissive. Easy! Never had I felt so submissive in my life. We squatted there plucking leaves like a friendly gorilla and watched a family with young'uns play around us. An extraordinary event!

———

Loading our antiquated, dead chest freezer, with its long-ago dented lid, into our van, we crossed into Kenya and drove to Nairobi. Locating a repairman, we had it examined and learned that it couldn't be repaired. Hauling it to a trash heap, we dumped it. That evening, we went to an elegant French restaurant for a special dinner. Inside the doorway, beside the hostess stand, stood our freezer, with its distinctive dent, purring away. An external compressor sat on the floor next to it.

———

Long distance flights offer the benefit of a stopover. We toured Cairo in the middle of one long flight from Uganda to the US. That massive city's temperature soared above one-hundred degrees. As I walked through the elbow-to-elbow bustle of the suk market, a cold glass of fresh strawberry smoothie abruptly appeared under my nose. Like a dying man in the desert, I drank it to the last drop in one fell swoop. Returning the glass to the hand that had presented it, the marketer immediately refilled the same glass, without washing, and thrust it upon another thirsty soul. "I'm gonna die!" rang loud in my head. How many people had drunk from the same glass that morning?

———

A wonderful variety of volunteers came to help us during Uganda's troubled days. One, a twelve-year-old boy, came with a group from Alabama to help with reconstruction after Idi Amin's overthrow. Showering in our guest room's tiny bathroom, he opened the shower curtain to face a cobra with head flared, swaying two feet away, under the sink. The term "blood-curdling scream" hardly does justice to what came next. Apparently, something had stunned that snake, as Jim captured and killed it easily. That young man had a story to tell! At the same house, just barely outside the gate, a cobra reared up from the pavement, spread its hooded head, and struck the front bumper of our VW Beetle. The Beetle won.

———

One Thanksgiving in Nairobi, we set a line of tables down the middle of the long back porch and cooked and cooked. Americans enjoy this holiday, getting together for a touch of home. I dyed the white African yams to look orange like our traditional sweet potatoes. We invited several Americans staying in local hostels away from their homes. We anticipated thirty. Preparation finished, the guests sat, and Jim gave thanks to God. We raised our heads, and behold there were several more people at the table than when we bowed our heads. Complete strangers to us, they heard by the grapevine of a Thanksgiving dinner at our house. They walked in, found chairs, and placed them at the table during the prayer.

———

A Baptist event of worship and teaching took place high on the backside of Mount Elgon, with Jim the invited preacher. At approximately seven thousand feet elevation, we experienced shortness of breath from the lower oxygen level as well as colder temperatures. Kampala, perched on Lake Victoria, sat four thousand feet lower. Jim, being the guest speaker, would have the last slot on the program. More people attended this event than could fit inside the building, so we gathered outdoors. As the sun went down, they built a fire. I tried to sit as close as possible, because by ten o'clock, three hours after darkness fell, I shivered. At eleven o'clock, the ladies served us supper. The host said that the food would keep me warm. I cupped both hands around the piping hot bowl with gratitude. Then, I looked into the steaming bowl and saw chunks of boiled sheep fat swimming in a pool of grease! "Lord, I'll get this food down in your name; you keep it down," a vital prayer of missionary life. Jim preached at midnight with great vigor, whether it was the Holy Spirit or the cold I didn't ask.

———

These moments caught our breath for sure, memorably so. Cannot Almighty God, as he moves himself into my day, my place, and this time, cause me to catch my breath? Think about it. Ponder the possibility through this day.

Hands Up!

I am the Lord; that is my name! I will not give my glory to another.

Isaiah 42:8

Have you ever heard those words—other than from an actor? Driving out of Kampala city center even on a normal day requires agility and nerves of steel. High school Driver-Ed did not cover the skill of dodging children, chickens, and goats, or the mandatory leeway to avoid bicycles laden with sacks of charcoal, huge stalks of green bananas, or even bed frames. Ladies with babies on their backs and bundles on their heads presented another challenge. Oncoming traffic, oblivious to the concept of lanes, moved into any available empty spot on either side of the road. Overloaded buses, so twisted from previous wrecks that you to see all four wheels at once, made it difficult to know their direction or their destination. Full attention required. This sets the stage for "Hands Up!"

This particular day on Gayaza Road, Jim focused completely on weaving the car forward without collision. He didn't notice the military vehicle that pulled up alongside of us. Our lady guest in the back seat emphatically announced, "That car beside of us! They're pointing big guns at us!" Our attention shifted. That insistent vehicle forced us off the road, sending pedestrians around us scrambling for their lives. Barked orders came,

"Get Out!" followed by "Hands Up!" The AK-47s, within inches of Jim's face, convinced him to get out. His hands went up. Twyla, our visiting mission volunteer, stood behind him, and her hands went up. I exited the car on the passenger side and stood a few feet away. My hands did not go up. Jim saw me out of the corner of his eye, and my open defiance horrified him. This was the second car stolen from me within a short time span, yet another of many stolen from our missionaries in Uganda. Enough! Not again! Indignation so gripped me that my hands would not go up. By God's mercy, these thieves' eyes focused on Jim, his keys, and the contents of his pockets. After a brief futile attempt to pull my wedding ring off my finger—the first time ever I gave thanks for the overgrown bump of gristle on my ring finger knuckle—they left us standing in a cloud of dust.

Do you remember the golden lamps with fluted edges, which held wicks feeding from a central pool of oil? Do you remember the source of that oil? Two living olive trees, one on either side, supplied the oil. God provided everything needed, continuously. "Not by might nor by power, but by my Spirit, says the Lord Almighty" (Zechariah 4:6).

Hands Up! forms an element of this truth. Suppose such a golden lamp lit my home. The ceiling in the center of my Virginia hexagonal house rises twelve feet, so let's say it could accommodate two olive trees. Now suppose that I am a *hands-on* type of person. Feeling responsible for the efficient running of our home, I regularly check the brightness of the lamp. I tinker with the oil, seeking a more fuel-efficient mix. One day I test canola oil in the lamp. Perhaps its heart-healthy benefit will increase lumens. Another day, after cooking a large roast, I have an exceptional amount of smooth lard. Rather than use it to feed the birds, why not try it as a cost-effective fuel in the lamp? Actually, neither canola oil nor the lard works at all, but still I think there must be something I can do or adjust to get a better result. The whole time, God implores, "Get your hands off my lamp!" However, too busy figuring, analyzing, scheming, and making plans, I fail to hear his voice. I miss the "Linda, Hands Up! Let *Me* take care of this!" and I thoroughly muddy the oil of the Spirit.

God promises that He will provide all requirements. However, we do have a part to play. We must submit to his authority, and yield ourselves to his plan. Allow him to do things his way. We must resist our natural tendency to take things into our own hands. *Letting go* grates against the grain of our core old nature, making it painfully difficult. Perhaps, the best way to keep our hands off the lamp is to stick them straight upwards towards him. If you pray Psalm 63 every evening, you know the line, "I will lift up my hands in your name." Lift your arms upward toward God in submission and worship. Hold your hands wide open, holding nothing, fully visible, hiding nothing, and up where they can't tinker with the oil. Hands Up! defines the posture of devotion that God longs to see from us every day.

One practical way I like to work this truth into my day involves a clean sheet of paper. God has blessed me with the most wonderful spouse, who rises long before I do. At the proper moment, he brings me a steaming aromatic cup of coffee. I prop myself up in the bed and simply inhale. I practice being still before the Lord. I lay out a blank pad of paper with a pen handy on my bedside table. Not speaking, not running ahead into the day, not diving into intercession or the asking kind of prayer, and not reading my daily Bible guide, I wait. Clearing and opening my mind and heart, I give God opportunity to speak. I allow him to select the topic.

The Holy Spirit and I savor the luxury of *chasing a thought* uninterrupted into the region that he chooses. Often, he leads me to chew upon a verse, slowly extracting a full flavor. The clean sheet of paper represents the day before me. It is God's to fill. I don't bring in the leftovers from yesterday. Each day awaits its own assignments. I don't first pencil in my aspirations for the day. I desire that God set the schedule, that he orchestrate the hours. Thoughts come, the page fills, and the time is fruitful. God loves such an opportunity. He has many ideas, all of them great. Sitting still and listening don't come natural. With intentional discipline, they do grow. Our hands long to tamper with the lamp and its oil—to do something! Hearing, resting, waiting, and trusting all improve with practice. Put your hands up!

Throughout the day, yield to him. God may alter any piece of my schedule anytime he wants to do so. No breech of etiquette, fear of embarrassment, or fear of offense should overrule his request. Traditions, appropriateness, and reputation can tie our hands. Indications that my hands aren't high up in the air of yieldedness may sound like this: "I'm taking the wheel! This is too scary. I might get hurt. What will people think? No God! Not now! Not that person! I know how to do this. I've got this one. I can't show up late for the next appointment. My current task is more important. Others count on me. Ask me again tomorrow."

Tape a picture of a cowboy with guns drawn on your bathroom mirror or at your desk. Let this picture remind you to ask, "Lord, are my hands up?" Make this part of your ongoing conversation. "Am I fiddling or fidgeting with something that annoys you?" Focus and listen intently, until you hear him say, "Hands Up!" and then obey. Jim urgently wanted to see me put my hands up that day on Gayaza Road. I know, because he later told me how appalled he was at my non-compliance. Is God any less appalled when he, the Master of the Universe, asks us to do something, and we refuse to listen? Do you suppose he grieves when we do hear his request, and yet we say, "No, I'm busy just now," or "How about doing it this way?" At least print Hands Up! in a large bold font and tape it to your mirror.

Hands Up! is a posture of devotion God would love to see from us every day. Hands Up! is the correct stance for being in the right place, at the right time, doing the right thing.

Bridgette from New Zealand

Saturday before Christmas, at my desk in Bible Way Correspondence School, I labored to finish a stack of work before the holiday office closure. Francis, a young guy perhaps thirteen years old, appeared at my desk. In his quiet voice, he asked me to visit a lady in Mulago Hospital. "Now?" "Yes." "It's not a good time for me." (Such a visit could never take less than an hour. In addition, hospital visits always lead to further trips to collect water or food from home, as the hospital had neither. Other requests would come, to wash the sheet and blanket, or to find a person who would provide basic care. Mulago was packed with hundreds of sick people and not much else.) Francis just stood there, waiting. Finally, I said, "Okay." We drove the few blocks, and then wound our way through hallways lined with patients on floor mats. We found Bridgette on a bed in a dark corner away from windows. Two shocks! She recently had surgery, serious surgery including a colostomy. With the scarcity of even soap, and more importantly, the rarity of antibiotics, major surgery wasn't a viable option—a dire outlook for sure. Second shock, she wasn't Ugandan. She came from New Zealand.

As part of the youth ministry, Francis visited patients randomly and offered to pray for them. He came upon Bridgette, who pleaded with him to find a foreign woman to come and talk with her. Thus began a series of visits. Astoundingly, she lived for three weeks. Her husband, a Ugandan professional, and their children—one white and one black—faithfully cared for her physical needs as best they could. They brought food and water, slept by her bed at night, and washed her clothes. But she had a load of emotional needs also. She knew that she would die soon. She couldn't face God. She believed that her multitude of sins prevented such a face-to-face encounter. With continual weeping, she confessed and confessed and confessed her sins to me. I tried to convince her of God's great love, mercy, and forgiveness by reading many New Testament verses to her. She couldn't accept this. Each day she told me of more sins from her past. I read more verses and explained their meaning. Still, she couldn't believe. Finally, I prayed with her that God himself would show her the reach of his forgiveness. The next morning, she called out to me before I reached the bed, with an energy I hadn't seen. "Linda, I think God answered your prayer! In the night, I heard, 'Though your sins are as scarlet, they shall be as white as snow.' What is that?" I showed her Isaiah 1:18 from the Old Testament. Joy overwhelmed her because of that night's experience. God had spoken to her. This time I was the one weeping. Again, I prayed the same, that God himself be the Convincer. The next morning, again Bridgette called my name as soon as I reached the ward doorway. She said, "Last night I heard, 'Just as I am without one plea, but that thy blood was shed for me.' What is that? Is it another verse?" No, not a verse but a song. I sang it for her and wrote it out for her to consider. Each night God did the same, speaking sometimes a verse or sometimes a song. One night, he used a child's song. This speaking may have happened for as many days as those days of her mournful confession. Whether God spoke those words out of her childhood memory, or whether he spoke them out of the clear blue heaven, I don't know. Clearly he spoke. He wanted Bridgette. Finally, she believed, accepted, and entered his peace. Then she asked me to bring letter paper, and she dictated letters asking forgiveness. One most precious communication went to her mother, who didn't know whether Bridgette lived or not. Three weeks after our first visit, she died in Jesus's arms. Months later, her mother, a praying believer, came to Uganda to meet Bridgette's family. She came to my desk at Bible Way School to meet me and to express thanksgiving to God for his mysterious ways in the restoration of her daughter. We corresponded for years.

I knew those visits to Mulago Hospital couldn't consume only one hour out of a day! This one lasted into eternity. I'm so grateful that God managed to pry my hands off that stack of exams to be marked. God can do wondrous things when we raise our hands up toward him. He can even manage to have us in the right place, at the right time, doing the right thing.

*** Pause for an Expansive Vista ***

Consider for a moment your expectation level. I hope you have the notebook and pen handy. Here come some significant questions. Draw a line down the center of a page, making two columns, one titled Evidence of Belief and the other Evidence of Unbelief. Scripture says that with God, all things are possible and that he is able to do exceedingly beyond anything we can imagine. Read it for yourself in Ephesians 3:20. Now ask yourself, do I believe this? This question requires thought. Continue the discussion with yourself to find evidences of your belief or of your disbelief. Fill in the columns on your paper. Do I attempt that which is impossible for man but is possible with God? When? List a specific instance. Don't skim over that line. It's a serious question. This question requires more than a yes-or-no answer. (During my daughter's student years, I learned to avoid yes-or-no questions. Otherwise, I learned nothing. The same applies here.) For fuller disclosure, try, "Why?" or "Why not?" until each column has several lines of evidence. Review yesterday's schedule. Which segment had the look of God? Which segment considered only personal goals, personal abilities, or the world's view of time? List these in your columns.

Remember a time when you felt the Holy Spirit prompted you to do something. How did you respond? Describe a time when you ignored him. Why? Think of an incident when you stepped into God's ability and out of your own ability. Revisit the details. Recall a situation when you thought your day was normal, that the mundane marked every hour, and then God opened your eyes to reveal his supernatural activity permeating your seemingly ordinary day. Continue to list the evidences for belief and the evidences for unbelief. Investigate and build a strong case for both sides. Let God speak through this exercise.

A workman stopped at my Virginia home, asking for directions. He noticed our African decor and asked questions about our time in Uganda. African traditional religion seemed to particularly interest him. So, without much thought, I gave a description of ancestral worship—the fear, intimidation, and bondage. He kept listening. Then he related how he had grown up with a religion that also venerated deceased relatives. The parallels were extraordinary. If I had known that fact earlier, I might not have spoken so freely. That day, God gave me a peek into his behind-the-scenes activity. A stranger's questions, curious about our décor, dealt with spiritual issues.

Is it possible that God has not designed even one barren moment for me? Is it possible there is something of eternal significance in my every moment? Is it possible the smallest detail can have a far-reaching domino effect within his comprehensive plan? Is it possible that God is such a multitasker that he can do this for every person of his creation at the same time?

Consider the Pharisee who paid Judas to betray Jesus. Could his greed have caused him to pay Judas only twenty-nine pieces of silver, keeping one for his own pocket? At the cross, could the centurion in anger have broken Jesus's legs as he hung on the cross, rather than simply piercing his side? Or consider the day Jesus sent his disciples to get a donkey for him to ride into Jerusalem on Palm Sunday. What if the donkey owner had refused to share his young animal? But they did not! Old Testament prophecy foretold every one of these details concerning Christ—the borrowed donkey, thirty pieces of silver, the scattering of his disciples, the scoffing, the piercing of his side, no broken bones, and much more. Despite the passing of hundreds of years, no detail was lost.

God is not only an extraordinary multitasker but also a masterful story-weaver. He can keep a story going for thousands of generations without losing a thread of the plot. We are simply one of a host of characters in his amazing story begun long before you and I lived. Each individual has a significant role to play. I ask you again, is anything too difficult for God? Is it possible my story is part of his story? If you have trouble embracing this thought, spend time in Matthew's first chapter and consider the genealogy of Christ. Consider the men and women in this line. Some are totally unknown elsewhere in Scripture. Some we expect, others seem unworthy, and some on the surface appear most ordinary, merely bystanders. Ask yourself a second time, is it possible that my story is part of his story? Take it as a hypothesis. Tentatively accept it and test it this next week. Discuss it with the One who determines truth. Ask him to prove it to you. Ask with the same persistence as a child in the backseat asking, "Are we there yet?" Watch for glimpses into the often hidden realm of God's activity.

God-absorption is the territory of great expectations, the great expectations necessary to enjoy a lifestyle of being in the right place, at the right time, doing the right thing. Check out John 14:21 and memorize this verse. He does love to show himself, to reveal his hand to those who are watching expectantly. God said in Jeremiah 32:27, "I am the Lord, the God of all mankind. Is anything too hard for me?" How do you answer this question? How expansive is your expectation level?

Leap Over the Fence

With my God I can scale a wall . . . He makes my feet like the feet of a deer.

2 Samuel 22: 30 and 34

Are you hungry, eager for the Lord? Are you delighted that he has chosen you to work with him in kingdom building? Has anticipation caused you to catch your breath? Are you standing ready with your hands up, giving him freedom to do whatever he wants? You are almost at the starting gate. There is one more preparation—deal with fences.

God-absorption is the territory of great expectations, the great expectations necessary to enjoy a lifestyle of being in the right place at the right time doing the right thing. Self-absorption is a territory where limitations loom large. No doubt at some point you have been told, "Don't put God in a box." The truth is God cannot fit into a box, but we surely can put ourselves into a great variety of boxes. We can and do box ourselves into some mighty tight quarters.

I have chosen to use the imagery of fences hemming us into cramped spaces. Fences are present in all our lives, and by nature, they define limits. They keep us from moving forward, appearing as obstacles. Some fences I build myself, but also other people build fences for me. Some fences are imaginary, only in my head, some are Satan's deception, but others are undeniably real. Circumstances such as tragedy, poor health, and childhood trauma can erect fences around our lives. We build fences to protect ourselves, to keep others out, or to allow us to say, "I can't." Our own sin is a fence that says, "I won't." Friends and enemies alike hem us in with fences, which say, "You cannot!" Life erects all sorts of fences, causing us to say, "I'm not able." In truth, the only fences that limit me are those I myself believe to be limiting.

The following images of physical fences can help us identify the spiritual fences in our lives that hinder our progress. Visualize each type of fence, white picket, or barbwire, before you read the description. Perhaps your neighbor has an evergreen hedge, so dwell on that hedge for a moment to allow the Spirit to speak from it. God-given images can instruct us. I'm sure Zechariah thought so.

<u>Whitewashed picket fences</u> prompt these rigid attitudes. I can't do that. What would people think? I can't be that spontaneous or demonstrative. I can't mix with that crowd, as it will spoil my image. It might offend someone. I must not be offensive. My style is clean, orderly, and predictably paced. I buy groceries on Tuesday, pray on Wednesday, and watch a movie on Friday . . .

<u>Electric wire fences</u> spark these wary concerns. I can't do that, as I might get my feelings hurt. That's way out of my comfort zone. It's not safe. My health requires eight hours of sleep and three square meals a day. I couldn't expose my children to such a risk.

<u>Barbed wire fences</u> prick me to withdraw. I can't. It is none of my business. My nose doesn't belong

in there, and if I go as you ask me, I might bleed. It's none of their business. Who do they think they are? Live and let live, that way no one gets hurt and everyone stays calm. Everyone stays on his side of the fence.

Invisible buried fences keep defeating my present with hidden issues of my past. Unforgiveness, old wounds, past sins—all of which I pretend are not there—keep popping up and entangling life. They damage relationships. They inhibit spontaneous response to God's requests.

Stacked split rail fences caution me to say, no. I'm too delicate, too unstable. I'm easily knocked off balance. Don't touch me. I've worked too long and hard for this look to try something new. All in its precise place keeps the world revolving smoothly.

Treated-lumber privacy fences say I'm not a socialite by nature. Faith is a private matter. It isn't respectable to hang out my dirty laundry for others to see. I'll see you at church, not in my home. Transparency is out. Don't get too close—arsenic in treated lumber is poisonous.

Chain link fences proclaim that life and relationships are complicated, especially when I am one person with Mr. A and a different person with Mr. B. I can't risk that. Everything might come unraveled. Don't involve me.

Stacked stone fences solidly declare that I am not able. I've tried it before and it failed. I always fail. Ask someone else. My health is weak. My sorrow is great. My load is heavy. My burdens are stacked too high. I'm a woman. I'm a man. I'm only a teen. (Aren't we glad that Jesus's mother Mary did not end the discussion with the angel Michael by saying, "I'm only a teen, and a virgin at that. This cannot happen!")

Trimmed evergreen hedges dictate that I don't have time. I must stay busy maintaining the status quo, my children's sports schedule, and my life's structure. I've always worked with children. My ministry would fail without me. People are counting on me. It takes most of my time to keep up relationships for my job. Running an efficient, clean, and respectable home consumes my energy and time.

Did you notice the prominence of *I* and *me*, the self-absorption?

Earlier I asked you to examine the strength of your belief that with God all things are possible. Now I ask you to examine yourself for fences, whatever causes you to say, "I cannot." Ask the Spirit to help you view these correctly. Are these fences true limitations, or rather are they designed to become stepping-stones to greater things? Can that great sorrow transform into comfort for others? Is that thorn an opportunity for God's glory? What role does Satan play in this limitation? Should you expose him as a liar and resist him? Is God not able to open unseen dimensions, expansive vistas, even within great burdens of daily responsibilities? Is not every experience of my past a potential tool for the future in God's hands? Do my perspectives match Christ's perspectives?

As mentioned earlier, making lists and setting goals can be useful, but they do not necessarily build good spirituality. They are tools, not the foundation upon which we stand. Likewise, fences can be useful tools, sometimes directive, and sometimes protective. They are not the sum total of the journey. Certainly, they are not the decisive last word in our choices.

God sets boundaries, not fences. He draws a line in the sand forming a boundary between light and darkness, setting a limit on evil. See Job 26:10—actually read the whole chapter. God won't allow Satan to tempt us beyond what we can bear. He allows no temptation to come without making a way of escape. Verify this in 1 Corinthians 10:13. No trial will come to us without its good purpose and even joy overflowing, as in James 1:2-3 and 12. His patience with sin does have limits, but his discipline is a corrective boundary to restore freedom, as explained in Hebrews 12:7-11. His boundaries transform us and set us free, free to do the impossible. They are for our good and his glory. God doesn't build fences that hem us into small, self-absorbed lives.

Great expectation is the air we breathe as his disciples. Fences are not prominent from our position of salvation, seated with Jesus in the heavenly realm, (Ephesians 2:4-6). What do you see, expansive vistas, or cramped corners? Are you God-absorbed or self-absorbed? Do you move toward God or away from him? Do you experience great expectations or serious limitations? Satan seeks to project every fence as a limitation, an impediment to being in the right place at the right time, doing the right thing. To *neutralize* means to destroy or counteract the effectiveness or force of something. Satan's slant on my fences, his incessant chatter, must be neutralized.

As a third grader, I walked miles on a country road to catch the school bus—well truthfully, I walked a mere half mile. Stretching along the last twenty-five yards, a fence surrounded a field with a big bull. Read *BIG BULL*, as a nine-year-old would. One morning that big bull stood alongside the fence. Fear gripped me. I refused to go one step beyond the corner post despite the pleadings of my younger sister. I cried and cried in fear, as I watched the bus arrive, my sister climb the steps and leave. I could not budge. A bit later, Dad pulled up, put me in the car, drove me past that threatening bull, and took me to school. My seriously flawed perception of fences needed correction. That fence limited the bull's freedom, but it should not have limited my movement. I did not understand it correctly as a boundary protecting me. I perceived it as a limitation, immobilizing me enough to miss the school bus.

The Rx for flawed fence perception includes big, frequent doses of God's Word. Meditate upon it. Imagine yourself in it. Use it as a sword to neutralize Satan's deceptions. Use it to take every thought in your own head captive, to make them obedient to Christ who always leads us forth into victory, (2 Corinthians 10:3-5). *It is okay to say, "I cannot," as long as we also say in the same breath, "but God can."* King David said, "Suddenly, GOD, your light floods my path, GOD drives out the darkness. I smash the bands of marauders, I vault the high fences. What a GOD!" (2 Samuel 22:29-30, MSG). Now is a good time to read and relish his song of praise in 2 Samuel 22.

Uganda had few phone lines, and finding a public pay telephone was not an easy task. To make a phone call required four of the largest, heaviest coins, about the size of silver dollars. We didn't have a phone our first years in the country, and it was common knowledge that any plan dependent upon a phone call was a bad plan. Our first stateside furlough after four years in Africa, we lived four blocks from Mom. One afternoon I needed to give her a piece of information and thus walked to her house, completely forgetting the phone. Today Uganda has by-passed landlines, going directly to cell phones. Men on bicycles talk on their cell phones. Ladies cooking rice over charcoal in mud-walled huts take dinner orders on their cell phones. In a land where only a short time ago it took several people to carry enough boxes of cash to pay for a major purchase, ordinary people now conduct bank transactions on their cell phones. Even villages with no electricity have a tall pole with a solar panel for charging cell phones. What a leap! An even greater leap is viewing our man-made fences from God's perspective rather than Satan's. What a transformation occurs when we leap over our *cannots* into all the possibilities that are his, into a realm beyond our wildest imaginations.

David knew that with God he could vault the high fences.

Read again Zechariah chapter two—yes, a second time! Notice the phrases "without walls" and "wall of fire." Identify the fence versus the God-infused boundary. How do these two images of truths affect the way you walk through this day?

The Devil's Hill

Benedict, a large effusive man, drove our mission's lorry, delivering relief supplies—like beans, blankets, seeds, rice, and sugar. He traveled to every corner of Uganda with these deliveries. One day a messenger arrived in our Kampala office to report that they found Benedict's truck on the side of the road between Mbale and Soroti, with his dead body inside the cab. Someone had shot him. No other information was available. No real clues, no real investigation, and no answers ever came. Friends brought his body to Kampala, but his family home was in a neighboring country, Kenya. East African culture demands burials take place on ancestral land. Their worldview has ancestors as intermediaries between a distant God and the living. We had to take Benedict's body to his ancestral home, and quickly, because embalming was unavailable. One friend phoned a message to the family to let them know of Benedict's death.

Crossing the border from Uganda into Kenya required specific dated documents. We all checked our papers. I had a travel document good for that day. No else did. They would apply. The process could be complete in twenty-four hours or it might take a week. No question, I would drive Benedict home. We found a young nephew to lead me to the village home place about two hours across the border. Not only did my heart feel heavy with sorrow, but also weightiness overlaid the whole event. A heavy dead body, quickly decaying, weighed down the truck bed. The unfamiliar route, the military road checks, and darkness weighed heavy in my mind, and the urgency of time weighed upon me physically. Leaving late afternoon, we reached the border at dark. Daytime border crossings held enough stress, but nighttime held additional unpredictability. I describe the art of crossing this border as a game of waiting, saying little, acting as if you have no other place to be, and not losing your temper. Eventually the guards gave up on receiving a bribe from us and called me into the office. After lecturing us on the lack of travel papers for the body, they allowed us to cross. This crossing took only an hour and a half, not too bad.

Darkness in the African countryside is deep, with no electricity to shoot a glow into the sky. We meandered along small dirt roads and footpaths until we reached the homestead at 11 pm. Upon sight of the vehicle, a trilling erupted from the crowd. The African trilling is a long high-pitched wavering sound, full of emotion, an unsettling sound for those not accustomed to hearing it. People flung themselves down on the road, thrashing about in front of my headlights. We inched forward until we reached the home. Swamped by the crowd, a man led me to a line of chairs in the yard. As my eyes adjusted to the dark, a grim scene unfolded. Our chairs formed a large circle facing the freshly dug grave. Wailing and trilling filled the air. My eyes and thoughts riveted upon the activity around and in the grave. Screaming, frantic, possessed men and women jumped down into the grave and out again. Obviously, Satan owned this hill and this night's event. A shiver went down my spiritual spine even as the cold of the night air made my physical spine shiver.

After a time—the passing of time that night defied quantification, as the intensity of the present moment pressed in hard—a man came to me and bent down to menacingly ask, "Why is there a bullet hole in Benedict's head?" I honestly thought that this would be my last night on earth—a catch your breath moment. Clearly, the earlier phone caller had withheld the fact of a violent death. I explained the details, as I knew them. The questioner left and did not return. The spiritual shivers began to trump the physical shivers, as I prayed through that night reminding myself that greater is HE who is in me than he who is in the world (1 John 4:4).

Shortly after dawn, a missionary colleague arrived. A most welcome sight! I had been way outside my comfort zone, way beyond the usual structures of my day. Fences shouting, "You cannot do this" encased almost every mile and every minute of this event. But God had been a wall of fire around me in enemy territory. What was his purpose in this beyond stretching my capacity for trust? I don't know, but I do trust that he was busy that night, building his kingdom of light in a place where darkness reigned. My testimony was so typically Ugandan. In almost every worship gathering, at least one person testifies, "God kept me through the night!" Traveling with the Lord, one should expect to be surprised. Boredom is not a stopover on his itinerary, nor is barrenness. Safety may not be either but adequacy is. God's activity may be hidden, but it is never absent. We are able to do whatever he asks regardless of what our fences say. Limiting fences are of man. With our God, who sets expansive, protective, enabling, boundaries, we can vault over the high fences.

Watch for Clues

Open my eyes that I may see . . . Open your eyes and look.

Psalm 119:18 and John 4:35

Do you remember my premise at the conclusion of the first section? God has a comprehensive long-term plan, which his people are to enact. He even restrains himself, waiting for us to do and be what he desires. God designs fruitfulness into every moment. Mystery and minutia fill his plan's agenda. His Spirit provides every requirement, as we step into his assignments. In other words, we God's people can be in the right place, at the right time, doing the right thing—consistently! I hope that page by page you more fully buy into this premise.

Since then, we have progressed along the pathway of heart, mind, and attitude adjustment, starting with cultivating a hunger for God. Moving into being delighted that he has chosen us for this task, we catch our breath at the awesome expectancy of his appearance. Throwing our hands up, yielding fully to his plan, we leap over every barrier that Satan erects across our path, as he attempts to stop this *foolishness*. We stand on the threshold of receiving specific assignments. Two needs remain at this point, eyes to watch for clues and ears to hear instructions.

Investigative TV shows proliferate. The search for clues and the piecing together of information, forensic science captures our imagination. Witness descriptions, fingerprints, personality profiles, DNA, motives, passions, sole prints, habits, quirks, cigarette butts, receipted shopping preferences, fabric fibers, timing sequences, and all manner of signatures left at the scene—everything is examined to determine the *Who*.

Just as seriously, we too look for clues but in reverse order. Criminal investigators use facts gleaned from the scene to reveal the who of the event. We, God's people, already know the Who. We use the facts of the Who—whom we know—to uncover and reveal his activity in our particular scenes, the places in which we find ourselves. We use our knowledge of him to determine the *what*.

We know the Who. The mystery, the question to be resolved, is what he is up to just now. What is he doing in this setting? What is my assignment? What is his agenda for me in this moment? So let's start with what we do know. Actually, we know much about him.

His Passions:

To have many children who look like Christ

To meet their needs and to give them abundant life

To make the unseen visible, to show himself

To receive glory, praise, worship

To speak with his children, to converse in prayer

To reveal truth and expose lies

To produce holiness, righteousness in sinners

To draw all men to himself so that no one would perish

To pour out love, peace, joy, kindness, self-control

To reconstruct broken lives

To love the world into his kingdom

His Preferences:

People over things

Rest over fretfulness

Fruitfulness over barrenness

Patience over hurry

Lowliness over arrogance

Today over tomorrow

Dependence over independence

Narrow over wide

Contentment over dissatisfaction

His Habits:

Blesses the unworthy, gives gifts, good gifts

Loves the unlovely, notices the downtrodden

Comforts the hurting, the grieving, and the rejected

Often speaks in a still small voice

Forgives easily, spends time with sinners

Weeps for the harassed and helpless

Sets people free, breaks bondages of darkness

Touches people, even the outcasts

Values every person, even widows, orphans, and strangers

Not bound to tradition, protocol, schedules, or conventional wisdom

Enjoys teaching truth through ordinary, everyday scenes

Has been known to turn over tables and wither an unfruitful fig tree

We do know the Who.

This knowledge enables us to gather plenty of clues
as to his activity around us.

*** Pause for a Scenic Overlook ***

Why clues? Why doesn't God just say up-front, loud, and clear what he wants me to do? Two basic reasons—the first has to do with me, the second has to do with him.

First, God's instructions are clear and precise more often than we are aware. My mind, full of distractions, worries, and self-absorption, keeps me clueless. My own disorderly lifestyle of fragmented priorities and *much ado about nothing* days keeps me in the dark. Even on a good day, I do well to catch a glimpse of the assignment God lays in my path. It looks like a scant clue to me, easily missed or ignored because of the way I live. Another sight-robbing problem is that the expectation of an assignment rarely surfaces in my thoughts, so I don't look for clues. Thus, it's rare that we recognize our God-designed task for the day.

Second, our God is a jealous God. He doesn't want to share us with any other person or thing. He waits until he is number one in my life. He waits for my full attention, much as I wait until I have the eye of a child before I give instructions. God isn't pushy. He waits until I eagerly want his plan. He waits until I seek and search for him, then he reveals himself and his assignments for me. As faith grows, my passion for God increases and he moves higher on my priority list. I shed distractions and focus more sharply. He reveals his activity in ways that grow my faith. If every communication appeared written in large letters, in bold font, faith disappears. If all is by sight, then there is no need for faith. Revelation by clues strengthens and stretches my faith. God communicates via clues designed to increase my desire and capacity to know him rather than any other god.

As I grow in faith through practice, clues become more and more obvious. My friend Shirley prays each morning, "Make me a blessing to someone today." That indeed happens to her all the time. She practiced looking and listening for his assignments for years. She doesn't doubt that there will be God-encounters throughout the day, and they do appear. The prophet, Isaiah, prayed, "Send me" and repeatedly yielded himself to the Lord's whatever, wherever, whenever. He obeyed all the way to walking around in his underwear for three years because the Lord wanted Judah to have an object lesson. (You don't believe me? Isaiah 20 confirms the story.) To no other prophet did God reveal more of his long-range plans than he did to Isaiah. The longer we walk with him in faith and obedience, the more clearly we discern his instructions. The closer a friend we become, the more he shows of his own heart, desires, and plans. Check out these verses, John 14:21 and Daniel 11:32. The scene before us is packed with God-clues, and he does want us to find them.

*** Back onto the original track ****

Now we return to eyes wide-open, seeking out clues as to the Lord's activity in our surroundings, his specific assignments. If I believe that God doesn't assign us even one barren moment, then I know that this moment holds fruitfulness. What could he have planned for me? Knowing much of his character, passions, and habits, I look.

** Perhaps he sets up a situation to further <u>shape my character</u> into the image of Christ with an abrasive to file off a rough edge, a test to strengthen a fruit of the Spirit, or a revelation to convince and convict me of sin.

** Perhaps God arranges a circumstance, whereby I can <u>make his name known</u> to a person who doesn't know him, placing me alongside someone who needs to be touched by a loving comment, or who needs a helping hand. Does he place me in the path of someone who needs to hear of Jesus as the source of my joy, peace, decisions, and pathway out of chaos?

** Perhaps God plans an extended time with someone who feels hopeless. He directs conversation such that common interests or histories appear. He plans for me to <u>refute the lie of Satan</u> that all is gloom and doom by sharing how Christ walked me through a similar situation.

** Perhaps he leads a parade of discouraged believers to cross my path today, having equipped me during my morning devotion with <u>encouragement for his people</u>. As I hold the door for a mom with five kids and a grocery buggy, I hear him prompting me to say, "Surely God has given me this opportunity at this door at this time to help you. He does love you. May I help you put these in the car?" As I hear of another's trail through the trials of chemo, the Spirit cues me to say, "God must still have a significant work for you to do on this earth, to keep you alive through this ordeal. I'll pray that he makes himself clear to you and shows you what it is."

** Perhaps he orchestrates paths on a wintery day, such that someone cold to the Gospel enters the office just as I do. With the weather being a non-offensive topic, I say, "I am so glad minus five degrees can't chill the joy I have in Christ!" Do you wonder where that comment originated? That *teaser* comment in the hands of the Spirit can <u>spark a hunger for God</u> in a cold heart.

** Perhaps God places someone, harassed and helpless, within my view, assigning me the task of <u>intercession</u> on his behalf. He desires my prayers so that he may bring resolution, change, or comfort into that life. If you doubt that he wants our prayer to accomplish his work, review the scenario in Revelation 8:1-5 where God waits to receive our prayers, then he purifies them in his holy fire and casts them back down to earth with dramatic results. Our prayers do effect change on this earth. He waits to hear, receive, and use our prayers.

** Perhaps he directs my path such that a person, object, or an event of beauty will capture my attention because he wants to <u>receive praise and worship</u> from me in this moment. Perhaps God hopes I will <u>proclaim his glory</u> through the expression on my face.

** ~~Perhaps~~ (strike that), for certain! God has a unique assignment designed for me in this spot, at this time. Spend time mulling that idea. Examine the clues.

God, the supreme multitasker, can do all this at once. What might he plan? If we will think for a moment, we do know what to look for. There is no reason for us to be clueless.

The crime scene investigator has a kit full of tools to glean information not visible to the eye: powders to dust for fingerprints, swabs to pick up DNA material, lights to expose blood residue, and a plethora of chemicals to uncover all sorts of hidden matter. They also have suspicious minds. We too should have suspicious minds. We rightly suspect God has an agenda, an intention, and a design for fruitfulness for every person in every place. We also have a sizeable tool kit for discerning his plans, for spotting his activity. Here are just a few of them. Use them to glean maximum information from your surroundings.

Stay on high alert, suspicious that God is on the move. Keep eyes wide open, looking to and fro. We stay alert for purse-snatchers, strangers, and terrorists, so why not be alert for God?

Speak to everyone, and make eye contact if you can't speak. Smile, indicating acceptance, love.

Practice observation. Look closely at individuals to discern stresses, needs, points for conversation, or provocation for prayer.

Appreciate others verbally. Compliments are rare, and they get one's attention. Simple civility can reveal clues. Civility requires intentional effort and time, a valuable expenditure.

Listen to those around you. Don't zone out into a magazine or your internal absorption with yourself; snoop in love. Ask God, "What are your priorities here?"

Offer help. Open doors, pick up dropped items. As you go to the Post Office for yourself ask if you can take other mail or do an extra errand. Make going the second mile a lifestyle.

Remember details such as names and faces. Call people by their name. Remember and comment on details of coworkers' children, activities, hopes, and concerns.

Soften schedules. Allow time for spontaneous conversations. Time your comings and goings to mesh with unbelievers. A frantic life, always in a rush, tells God that you are not available.

Alter routines to increase observation skills, alertness. Even a simple change can open our eyes: sit or park in a different place, walk a different route, order a different menu item, dress out of character, change the picture on your desk.

Break out of *holy huddles* to mix with outsiders. Give God the opportunity to encounter a new person through you. We shouldn't spend all our time with like-minded people. Jesus didn't.

Ask questions, non-threatening ones, and listen intently to the answers. Ask for opinions and listen without judging or even without stating your own opinion. "I'm in a quandary, what do you think?"

Pray with eyes open. Lift to the Lord what you see and you will be amazed at what you begin to notice just inside the invisible realm. Wide-eyed prayer awakens discernment.

Build these tools into your lifestyle. They require no more time than dusting a room for fingerprints does, and they will uncover much of significance. Pray and read Scripture before stepping into the day. It will clean your spyglass and keep your tool kit at hand. Another tool, as effective as a magnifying glass, is to walk through the day in an attitude of worship and thankfulness. Vision will improve greatly. Don't discount or ignore any small thing. Remember this was God's instruction to those rebuilding the temple and the walls—one stone at a time. Now, read Zechariah 14:20-21, the last two verses of his book. God designates even the bells on the horses and the kitchen cooking pots as "Holy to the Lord." For someone who regularly uses cooking pots, this encourages me. Even my cooking pots, he uses to accomplish his plan. Every mundane part of my day, God wants to use for his glory. The small things are his discipleship program. Become an avid seeker of clues. Remember the Who you know, and look for his likely activity. Let's be the Sherlocks who notice every tiny detail, not the Watsons who express dismay at what they missed.

She touched us!

In the late '80s, photographers and journalists came to document Uganda's AIDS crisis during the early years of this disease. They, an intense bunch, focused on making the most of each encounter, and took more pictures in one day than I have in my entire life. Even now, when the sun begins to soften from its direct midday harshness, we say, "Hop to it. This is a Pinneo moment." Professional photographer Joanna Pinneo anticipated the right light for these black faces, and when it came all else ceased. She went to work, making the most of every opportunity. After photographing two ladies with AIDS, she thanked them with a hug. Their entire bodies expressed shock. In Luganda, which Joanna didn't understand, they said, "She touched us. No one touches us. She hugged us!" God certainly knew how to make the most of that moment.

Many people with AIDS found acceptance and love in Christ because of such a touch.

MKs are great!

Bible Way Correspondence School enrollments increased at our booth in the open-air market when Kristen's long straight blond hair was on site. As she moved into her pre-teen years, she resisted the stroking of her hair by strangers, but until then we capitalized upon it. The Ministry of Health initiated a polio vaccination campaign in Kampala. They chose an impoverished neighborhood as a trial location, a neighborhood where we hoped to start a new church. Evil rumors regarding the vaccine spread across the city. "Our enemies poisoned the serums. Children who take the vaccine would suffer long-term consequences." These rampant rumors would likely cause a low turnout for the vaccine. Parents were afraid to allow their children to receive the drops. Vaccination day arrived. Four of our young missionary kids (MKs) walked into this slum area without us adults in sight, though we were not far. They stepped into doorways of homes, offering to carry babies to get the polio drops. The shock factor of four young white kids in their house caused parents to agree. What a day that was! Older toddlers followed our children as they carried their younger siblings.  Those four MKs looked and moved like short pied pipers. I will never forget the sight of those young white faces in a sea of black. Exuberant exhaustion aptly described our condition by the end of the day. That neighborhood had the highest turnout for the whole of Kampala city, and a church stands there today. God had a good plan, and this time we caught the clues.

Listen and Hear

He, who has ears to hear, let him hear.

Mark 4:9

With spy kit at hand, I hope you notice an increasing number of clues strewn throughout your day. However, these clues may refuse to coalesce into a clear assignment, too many possibilities, too much information. Fractured observations, a glimpse here, a glimmer there, gleaned as we scurry through our routines, don't make sense. They don't give us clear understanding or direction. To extract meaning, significance, and personal assignments, we must not only be alert to the externals, but also we must be alert to the internals. Listen. Listen for the still small voice of the Spirit. And yet, simply listening is not enough. We must *listen and hear*.

How many times did Jesus say, "Let he who has ears hear" to those who listened to his words but still did not get it? They did not hear. Let's look at this issue of listening and hearing. Open to Mark 4, a familiar story. Read verses 1-13. Jesus prefaced his story with "Listen!" He concluded, "He, who has ears to hear, let him hear."

Some listened to Jesus tell this story as a beautiful illustration of the order of nature. The seed nourishes the birds, the soil provides growth, and thorns insure survival of the fittest—a glorious circle of life. This story made them feel all warm and fuzzy. Others thought that obviously this man studies agriculture. How refreshing to hear from one who speaks in such earthy tones, not in religionese, or with grandiose airs, trying to impress. This story, rooted in the soil of life, tells me that he knows his farming. I wonder if he would look at my land and suggest how to increase production. Did they really hear? They did not. They listened but without understanding. Jesus describes them as "ever hearing but never understanding."

Insiders, those inside the kingdom of God, can understand spiritual instructions. Those outside of Christ's kingdom find it difficult to grasp spiritual implications. Insiders have the secret to the kingdom. They have the indwelling instructor, the mystery revealer, and the code breaker—the Holy Spirit who interprets the Word. To the Outsiders Jesus says, "Why is my language not clear to you? Because you are unable to hear what I say. You belong to your father, the devil," (John 8:43-44). Read through verse 47. Insiders, those who have turned away from Satan's kingdom to enter God's kingdom, can *hear*. Consider a student attending a lecture, who sits with his back toward the speaker. Will he not hear much better if he rotates his chair to face the lecturer? An about face toward the speaker, a change of direction—repentance—opens ears.

A hungry pursuit of God precedes a turn away from all that Satan offers. The U-turn is precursor to the hands up of self-abandonment. This progression culminates in ears that *hear*. No Hands Up! limits assignments, not because there are no assignments but because they aren't understood. The above listeners received a story about seeds, and they perceived nothing more. To the Insiders Jesus says, "To you have been given the secret of the kingdom." Consequently, stories about everyday things reveal truths from the invisible realm, truths of divine instruction. God wraps his kingdom truth, his guidance, within the ordinary scenes and stories before us. He speaks through today's encounters, conversations, sights, smells, and sounds. Those on the inside hear him.

In the mall, you watch an older woman entertain a three-year-old. What do you *hear*? A joyful scene of Grandma's day with grandchild to be enjoyed at a distance? A sigh of dismay that yet another parent has abdicated their responsibility, leaving child rearing to grandparents? An irritation at the noise? An inner urging to join them? Perhaps a God-designed assignment unfolds in a friendly conversation. "It surely does take a bundle of energy to keep pace with this beautiful child." A little chitchat follows as you admire the child. "I've heard it said that it takes a village to raise a child, but actually it takes God. I could never have made it through child rearing myself without Jesus's wisdom, strength, and mercy. I hope you have him yourself for this precious little one."

What do you hear?

You coincidentally meet your neighbor at the mailbox. What do you hear?

You notice an anxious person in the cafeteria. What do you hear?

A coworker frets, dreadfully behind with a tight deadline. What do you hear?

Ambulance lights flash at the neighbor's home. What do you hear?

As you wait for an oil change, the counter attendant personifies boredom. What do you hear?

Gossip of *so-and-so's* daughter's arrest circulates? What do you hear?

A big sports event arrives, and you plan to watch it alone? What do you hear?

Are you listening? Does your hunger for God cause you to strain with alertness to hear? Have you turned away from all that fills Satan's kingdom to fully face Christ so that your spiritual ears can hear? Are your hands up ready to receive whatever he offers? Are you facing the Speaker?

What hinders hearing?

External noise: radio, TV, too many people, or music—even constant praise music.

Internal noise: worry, fantasy, schemes, *what ifs* and *if onlys*, and ruminating on the past.

No expectation: no anticipation that God speaks, no listening, our distracted faces turn away.

Busyness: talking, lack of silence, electronic devices, or continuous Facebooking.

Mislabeling: isn't God. Lack of sleep, too much caffeine, or spicy food affects my brain.

No desire: schedule set, too busy, other goals, competing hungers, life clogged with sin and self.

What enhances hearing?

Focus upon Christ, the Speaker, and be slow to speak.

Call the name Jesus as prayer multiple times in your day.

Ask "What!?" followed by a pause. Make it a habit.

Place reminders in your pathways. Tape "What's happening?" in unexpected places.

Relax the schedule to make time for listening. Park in a distant space, or sit alone for lunch.

Set aside a time and dedicate a place for conversation with the Lord.

Be faithful in quiet time with God early, before the day commences.

Take an extra walk to the copier for a mini God-conversation.

Reduce unnecessary distractions, the noisy ones, whether external or internal.

Stairwells are usually quiet, so walk and listen rather than ride the populated elevator.

Frequently ask God, "Am I missing anything here?' Then look and listen.

Schedule a day of solitude and quiet retreat to sharpen hearing. Add fasting.

Strengthen the two-way conversation in the back of your head, called prayer without ceasing. Remember conversation with God isn't a monologue. Allow plenty of space for his response.

As noisy as our world is, often the greater noise pollution is internal—our own thoughts. Examine where you spend your mental time and energy. Is it a hospitable place for God's still small voice? We can have the mind of Christ (1 Corinthians 2:16). Ask him to take your thoughts captive to Christ as in 2 Corinthians 10:5. Deliberately set your mind on things above (Colossians 3:1-2). New mental pathways can form, overriding even the most well worn, hardened trails. As multitaskers and multithinkers, we rarely have only one stream of thought in our heads at any one time. With effort and practice, we can develop an ongoing dialogue with God in the back of our heads, even as we converse orally with others. It is possible and worth the effort. Ask the Lord to make 1 Thessalonians 5:17 a reality in your mind, actually deep within your soul. Conversation with God yields far greater profit than conversation with my own self.

Our God communicates. The whole sweep of Scripture and history confirm this.

He has plenty to say, if only he can find a hearer.

Quiet!

In 1979, Milton Obote overthrew the tyrannical rule of Idi Amin. Jubilation reigned. (Not seeing the future can be a blessing. Enjoy the day at hand.) The world beyond Uganda knew of the misery and devastation inflicted upon the country and its people by Amin. The National Geographic covered the expulsion of 60,000 Asians in 1972, and by 1974, several magazines reported on the 90.000 people killed during Amin's first two years of rule. We lived in Jinja, Uganda's second largest town, during Obote's coup. We soon learned that this change did not bring about easy days of law and order, free of chaos.

The news of Obote's coup ousting Idi Amin compelled many to come to help rebuild Uganda. Within a couple of months, six amazing college students moved into our house for the summer months to distribute donated medicines across the country. We purchased all our food in

Kenya because the official Ugandan exchange rate made one tiny tomato cost $1.50. As the six students arrived, we drove to Nairobi—remember it's twelve hours away—with a chest freezer in the back of a van. Filling it with food, we plugged it in for two days to freeze, and then drove back into Uganda.

Next, came four young adults for a year's volunteer ministry to restart Bible Way School, develop water resources, and do whatever needed done. They moved in next door. After eight years of Amin, our mission had dwindled to two families, and one left on stateside assignment shortly after this Obote coup, leaving an empty house attached to ours. It became a dorm for the next year. Our house resembled a dorm most of that year too. Many, eager to participate in the rebuilding of Uganda, arrived to discover that there were no hotels or restaurants operating in town. One memorable evening, a group of nine, all strangers to us, arrived at nine. "Could we sleep and eat with you?" They ate a simple meal of stew and banana bread. We had baked twenty loaves of banana bread the day before. Spreading out across our living room, they slept. Extraordinarily busy days!

The tons of donated medicines, which the six students would distribute, arrived first in Nairobi. Then, Jim maneuvered them through customs and reloaded the crates onto train boxcars to travel to Uganda. Essentially, Jim moved to Nairobi to accomplish this process. I remained in Uganda to coordinate the distributions. We had acquired several vans for this purpose. The students, sent out two by two, delivered medicines and Bibles to every corner of Uganda. Those guys did an astounding job amid chaotic circumstances. For a driving break, they stopped at schools and asked the headmaster to line up the students for an impromptu health clinic. After popping a de-worming pill into each mouth, they led an old-fashioned *Sword Drill,* testing who could find verses the quickest and awarding the winners with Bibles. Exhilarating and challenging days!

With the rousting of Amin's army, abandoned guns were everywhere. Everyone and his brother, and his sister, had guns. They provided great fun, great power, and great trouble. No one went out after dark. Obote's men found authority invigorating and addictive, ever requiring more. Military roadblocks increased in hostility. Orchestrating volunteer activities held increasing perplexity and tension. We prayed unceasingly, especially for the traveling students. Within the next twelve months, Uganda experienced three coups and presidents: Muwanga, Lule, and Binaisa. Vehicles were stolen. Our lorry driver was shot dead. Exhausting and traumatic days!

One Sunday in the midst of this hyper-activity, I drove a circuit, through the villages surrounding Jinja, dropping our volunteers at several churches as their guest preachers. Alone on my way back into town, I stopped at a roadblock. A soldier ahead of me ran toward me with his AK-47 assault rifle, aimed and fired, the sound jarring the air. Without a doubt, a catch-your-breath-moment! He shot a Maribu stork standing outside my window on the road's shoulder. The officiating soldier thought my consternation was hilarious fun, and in the process of checking my papers, he grabbed my breast. I immediately sped away praying that the Maribu shooter did not have more bullets.

Reaching town safely but rattled, I decided not to go to church, opting for a quiet moment instead. I drove to the Source of the Nile Park, a beautiful spot where the Nile River begins its journey north out of Lake Victoria. Bougainvilleas, palm trees, birds of paradise and the sounds of water would soothe my soul. I couldn't remember when I last refreshed in a peaceful solitary moment. I sat on the grass, actually laid on it, breathed deeply, and prayed the prayer of the blind beggar, "Lord Jesus Christ, have mercy on me." As I said earlier, enjoy the moment at hand for we don't know the future. A man walked up beside me, yanked the watch off my arm, and grabbed my purse, which held my Bible and my passport! I never wore a watch again in Uganda—not a bad thing in the long run. I could do without the watch, but it was unacceptable to be without a passport. I chased him to no avail. Distraught, I started the tedious process of reporting to the police to get official documentation verifying the passport's theft. Then the process of applying for a replacement could begin. Two days later, the purse turned up and the finder took it to the police station. I got a message to come to the police station to get the bag, which still held the Bible and passport, though, no money. As I arrived with great relief, the Captain called me into his office. He handed me the passport and commenced a long lecture. "None of this drama was necessary, nor would our time have been wasted, if you had not gone to the park to meet a man while your husband was out of the country!" Dumfounded, I wanted to flee, but I had to wait graciously to the end of his harangue.

It isn't possible to put into print my state of mind, spirit, and soul. As if I did not have enough stressors in my life, I needed this humiliating lecture! (Actually, additional serious issues roiled those days, but not everything should be written on paper.) I managed to contact Jim in Nairobi with "Come get me. I am going to lose it." He came and took me out of Uganda. I felt relief just riding across the border into Kenya. Jim left me at a conference and retreat center on the edge of lush tea fields. I walked those fields. I wish I could say that the Lord refreshed me immediately.

Not so. I railed against him. So what about mercy? Where is it? Where are you? Is this chaos of your doing? I informed him of every detail.

"Quiet!" Loud and clear, I heard that shout, emanating from somewhere above the acres and acres of green tea bushes. "Quiet!" It was a shout. It was a demand. It was God. It got my attention. Then in the Spirit's still small voice, "Why do you say, Linda, that your way is hid from me? Why do you assert that the justice due you escapes my notice? Do you not know? Have you not heard? The everlasting God, the Lord, the creator of the earth does not become weary or tired. His understanding is inscrutable. He gives strength to the weary, and to him who lacks might he increases power. Though youths grow weary and tired, and vigorous young men stumble badly, yet those who wait for the Lord will gain new strength; they will mount up with wings like eagles, they will run and not get tired, they will walk and not become weary." He spoke to me in his language, from his Word. These verses end Isaiah's chapter 40. Some years earlier, I had memorized that chapter for a speaking assignment.

The discussion ended, or more honestly, the ranting monologue ceased. The bloating of stress, anger, and dismay drained away. I found myself ready to return. Nothing on the ground had changed. Four more coups and presidents lay ahead, as did more car thefts and hostile roadblocks. The AIDS epidemic hadn't even started, but it would sweep the nation. What changed? Why could I now return? God adjusted my vision, my heart, and my hearing. We were on the same page, and I could move forward one day at a time once again. He spoke and I *heard* him.

Just Do It–Consistently

"Amen" is spoken by us to the glory of God.

2 Corinthians 1:20

The Premise

God has an agenda for this day.

He waits for us to participate.

Mystery and minutia are hallmarks of his activity.

The oil pipeline flows with the Spirit's adequacy.

The Process

Come Hungry

Delight in Being Chosen

Catch Your Breath

Hands Up!

Leap Over the Fence

Watch for Clues

Listen and Hear

The last step

Just do it, consistently. Say "Amen" to the "Yes" of Christ.

> "For no matter how many promises God has made, they are "Yes" in Christ. And so through him the "Amen" is spoken by us to the glory of God." – 2 Corinthians 1:20

> "Whatever God has promised gets stamped with the Yes of Jesus. In him, this is what we preach and pray, the great Amen, God's Yes and our Yes together, gloriously evident. God affirms us, making us a sure thing in Christ, putting his Yes within us. By his Spirit he has stamped us with his eternal pledge—a sure beginning of what he is destined to complete."

> – 2 Corinthians 1:20-22, MSG

> Note: *Amen* means emphatic agreement.
> Yes, let this be so! I agree! Let's do this!

> God's Yes and our Yes together.

The key to consistency hinges on the word *this*—this place, this time, this person, this voice, this encounter, and this job. This is the day the Lord has made. The only moment for which we are responsible is this one. We expend too much energy on tomorrow and the bigger things to come. While peering into the future, we miss today's assignment. The long-term *whats* of our lives have such a firm grip on us that we stumble over God's agenda for this moment. We expect Christ's return when the trumpet sounds, but we do not expect him when the phone rings. Consistency comes as we step into *this* day with an expectation to see God and a plan to do and be whatever he asks. Tomorrow, and the past for that matter, doesn't hold as powerful or as ominous an influence as we think it does. Consistency comes when I awake each morning with the declaration, "Amen! Let's do this! Yes!"

Enhancers for Discernment

I am your servant; give me discernment that I may understand.

Psalm 119:125

Do you still think you will not recognize what God wants when he asks?

To enhance clarity, incorporate these principles into your journey.

All about Him, Not Me

Examine the discussion in your head. Do you hear I/me/my or you/yours? "God, what in this day will make me comfortable, or fit my style, my timetable, my budget?" "God, what are you doing today, and how may I fit your purpose, and your schedule and accurately reflect your character?"

Learn God's Language

God speaks his Word. The more Word I know, the richer our conversations flow. Significant conversations with the Lord grow out of saturation in his Word through meditation, private and corporate study, and through hungering after every verse in both Old and New Testaments. Enroll in God's language course. Study the Bible itself, not only what others say about it. Go direct. As Donald G. Barnhouse says, "The shortest route to understanding the Bible is the acceptance of the fact that God is speaking in every line." Learn his language well.

When I knew only ten words of Luganda, people tired quickly with my, "My name is Linda. What is your name? I stay in Kampala. Where do you live?" Vocabulary had to increase. With ongoing usage, words I thought I knew took on increasingly complex shades of meaning. Eventually we learned that when one said, "My father died," it could mean any of a host of male relatives. So an employee could tell us, "my father has died" multiple times without Jim firing him for lying to us. Or when driving with a guide to an unknown location, repeatedly we heard the destination described as *just there*. However, we came to understand that *just there* did not indicate nearness, but only that it is still ahead. Our daughter, arriving in Uganda as a two-month-old baby, had similar English issues. She grew up speaking *Special English* as used on Voice of America radio, a version devoid of slang and colloquialisms. Years of colonial rule by Britain gave Uganda its English, so they weren't familiar with American English. We dropped all those confusing American figures of speech, in the attempt to communicate well. As a toddler visiting her grandmother, Jaja, in Virginia, Kristen came to me crying, "Jaja says that I am *pulling her leg*, and I'm not even close to her leg." She knew the words but not this meaning. As relationship matures in time, knowledge, and intimacy, conversations carry deeper intimations. Jim can say, "I quit my Bank Americard job," and immediately a burst of romance flows over me. It makes no sense to others, but this phrase goes back to our early days of marriage, when we thought we needed more money. He took a second job, and we barely crossed paths. I remember well the night he walked in at 11:00 p.m. and said, "I quit my Bank Americard job!" Marriage blossomed.

If we want to hear—really hear—what our communicating God has to say, we must become fluent in his language, his Word. Shortcuts don't exist. You can't bypass his Word and expect to be on the same page with God. Without it you will miss-hear and without God's in-put you will wander into chaos. "My name is Linda. What is Your Name?" doesn't suffice.

Seeing the Whole Picture is not Necessary

I don't need to understand the full thrust of a circumstance or an assignment before acting. One aspect of our freedom in Christ releases us from the debilitating immobilization caused by the need to see and understand every detail ahead of time. Arrogance demands full understanding, as it requires that God explain himself to me. Disobedience says, "Tell me where this goes, then I will decide if I go or not." We may ask why, but we don't camp there. God creates good plans, complete down to the tiniest detail. We see the knots and thread ends on the back of the tapestry. He sees the emerging pattern. Likely, we wouldn't believe his plan if he did reveal it. If you still struggle with the need to see and understand more, review the section on mystery back in the Premise section. Ask the Lord to give you a heart of faith to go wherever he leads without understanding the succeeding steps. Faith and sight struggle to coexist.

Nor is Recognition

Testify to what *God* has done. Tell of *his* wondrous deeds. The pure in heart will see God. Hunger for recognition does not reside in a pure heart. It blinds us to God and his activity. If I claim the glory, I rob God. The more of me seen, the less God is visible. Deny selfish ambitions and God can accomplish amazing feats. The thirst for honor obscures our vision of God. The hunger for recognition sneaks up on us. Practice vigilance.

Shed Dead Weights — *What Ifs* and *If Onlys*

Fear and anxiety thrive in Satan's territory, but we don't live in his realm. God presents you with an assignment. You respond, "but what if _____." Fill in the blank. Now examine it. Zechariah 2:5 says, "And I myself will be a wall of fire around it, declares the Lord, and I will be its glory within," speaking of his people. Whatever comes through to you has passed first through the Lord, our wall of fire. God allows only that which matures you and moves you toward his purposes. Repeatedly Scripture tells us that he forms a hedge of protection around us. We are in Christ and he is in us. Fear, anxiety, and what-ifs, do not have to weigh us down. Nor should regret, feelings of inadequacy, or past experiences impede us. God presents you with an assignment. You respond, "but if only_____." Fill in the blank. Now examine it. Review Isaiah 43:1-21, and 2 Corinthians 2:14 and 3:3-6. As you examine your responses, can you see that both evidence self-absorption? "I cannot!" "I am not worthy!" Both statements are true. Accept these truths as a profitable position of humility. But don't allow inertia to claim you. Quickly rejoice that Christ can when you cannot, and that he is worthy when you are unworthy. God provides adequacy, very well actually.

Manipulation is Out

If I concern myself with working the circumstances, no longer do I stand in the position of humility. To *wait* on the Lord takes great strength of character. He wants our availability. God doesn't need us to force situations or change the arrangements. With practice, we recognize the difference between moving in our own strength and moving in his strength. Be alert, as we can slip easily out of that energizing spot.

In the fall of 1974, Jim and I returned to Virginia from seminary in Texas. We drove an aging VW Beetle, packed tight with suitcases and laden with weighty boxes of books on the roof rack. Bikes and lawn chairs hung on the rear rack. Driving straight through from Fort Worth to Christiansburg in rotating shifts, the journey seemed to stretch on forever. Once, as Jim slept and I crept up a long hill, I made an amazing discovery. As I edged *too* close to the tractor-trailer in front of us, the VW experienced a burst of energy. We moved faster than on any other portion of the journey, and I barely depressed the accelerator. The truck's wind drafts whipped around us and engulfed the car, pulling us along in his strength, using his gas and not our own. The driver wasn't happy with me. I recognized  this when he pulled off on the shoulder of the road and emphatically motioned for me to go away. It was great while it lasted.

If your walk with God grows increasingly laborious, or if your peace and joy diminish, check for manipulation. Whose strength moves you? Manipulation exhausts. The cure calls for you to throw up your hands and stop tinkering with the oil in Zechariah's lamp.

So are Line Item Vetoes

Obedience is obedience-in-full. Obedience becomes disobedience, only slightly disguised, if we say, "I'll do everything except this small piece, except for that person, except not right now." No matter how tiny, disobedience in any area puts us at odds with God. Obedience loosens the grip of sin and gets us back on the same page with God. Eliminate line-item vetoes.

Lay Down the Tape Measure

Read Zechariah 2:1-5. Zechariah saw a young man moving out with a tape measure in his hand. This man, excited about the growth prospects for Jerusalem, wanted to quantify it for analysis, getting it down in precise figures. But one angel sent another angel to go stop that young man, explaining that the Jerusalem he sees is an inaccurate perception. For starters, it won't have stone walls to be measured in meters or feet. Nor did he own any tool that could measure the vast number of people who would populate the city. His measuring line wouldn't do. Beware of trying to quantify results in your own terms.

It takes a little getting used to, laying aside the tape measure. God's activity doesn't have typical parameters. The who, the where, the when and the how may not look as we expect. Our common standards and measures are unable to evaluate his plans, the likelihood of his activity, and even the success of accomplishment. We must leave the measuring, the determination of success, to God.

I like to use a stereogram with its hidden 3-D image to illustrate our perception of the kingdom of God. At first glance, it seems a chaotic collage of multicolored geometric patterns. But if you hold the page at precisely the right distance, squint your eyes just so, and tilt your head sideways a degree or two, another image pops into view. This image, unseen by the casual viewer, jumps out of the chaos. The young man envisioned walls of stone around the city. Whereas with the correct adjustments, he might have seen the flaming walls of Christ's holiness. Elisha's servant did see the flaming chariots in 2 Kings 6:16-17. Much more than a hidden 3-D picture, God's kingdom permeates all that our natural eyes casually observe. In truth, his kingdom, though often unseen, rules every other kingdom. The point of the stereogram wasn't the chaotic geometric pattern, but rather the hidden picture. If the hidden image never appeared, the stereogram's purpose failed. If I travel through my day and only see the chaotic, though colorful, patterns of the world, I haven't seen God's picture. Most of our tools lack the capability to detect God's hidden kingdom, and they are woefully inadequate for measuring it. For this, we rely upon the indwelling Holy Spirit, the Word of the Lord, and the body of Christ.

Do Keep the Plumb Line

Measure yourself against that which is reliable. Saturation with the Word and sensitive listening to the Spirit's leading yields reliable measures. Welcome conviction and exposure of sin, and quickly confess it. Stay in close, accountable fellowship with the body of Christ. Practice! Practice! Practice! You will grow better. Zechariah 4:10 instructs us to gladly embrace the small tasks. It also reads, "Men will rejoice when they see the plumb line . . ." The plumb line represents God's truth, his accurate measure for everything we face. Lay aside the tape measure, but do keep the plumb line.

Personality Type is a Non-issue

Don't even bother trying to tell God why he cannot use someone like you. The whole sweep of Bible characters proves you wrong. Does your voice sound worse than, are you uglier than, or is your stubborn streak stronger than the donkey God used profitably with Baalam in Numbers 22?

She was the one

The disease AIDS began to impact ministry in Uganda long before it had a name. Considering it a curse, family members abandoned sick relatives in distant banana fields to die. Witchdoctors prospered by offering expensive cures for this curse, offering false hope. Fear and dread gripped many. The topic was taboo. In the greatest of privacy and assurance of secrecy, some admitted to us that they had the HIV virus.

During this same time, a group of twenty-plus believers prayed for spiritual awakening in our city. The prayer for spiritual awakening and AIDS coincided. No tape measure could anticipate such a meshing. In the light of AIDS and its opportunity for the gospel, this praying group sought a person willing to openly speak of their HIV status to Kampala Baptist Church, a highly educated, English-speaking, urban, and university related church. All of us in this prayer group knew church members who had AIDS, but they would not reveal it, publicly. We prayed and prayed asking God for the right person to propel the church into action, for the right face to convince its members to embrace those suffering, and for the right story to compel them to demonstrate the love of Christ. We asked many. They refused. One young woman, an illiterate, non-English speaking, destitute, single mom, with a face gaunt from the disease and the tell-tale purple spots on her skin—so unappealing in her poverty—repeatedly asked to share with the church the impact of Christ upon her life. We repeatedly said, "No, not here, not yet." The Lord prevailed and convinced us that Zawedde was the one, the right one.

Sunday morning Zawedde, visibly shaking in apprehension, stood before the congregation of three hundred. Daudi the pastor stood beside her to translate her Luganda into English. Daudi, tall and energetic in his sharp suit and highly polished shoes, presented quite a contrast. Her testimony, clear and compelling, held attention. Christ rescued her and transformed her life. She told of the amazement and joy beyond comprehension, which now filled her life because God chose her, in her pathetic state of sin and HIV, to receive his love. "You think there is nothing good about me, but I now have Christ. The only good in me is Christ." Toward the end of her story, she began to tremble and falter from the strain. Daudi stepped closer, placing his arm around her shoulders to steady her. The church quietly but audibly gasped. I heard it. You do not touch someone with AIDS. Culturally men don't touch even healthy women in public. In that *moment of the gasp*, God did his work. The truth of the reach and touch of Christ's love stretching across the abhorrence of all our unworthiness became visible as Daudi and Zawedde stood before

the congregation. The church body recognized their assignment. From that day, they moved forward into it, embracing these untouchables with the love of Christ. The Cup of Cold Water ministry began and continues today. Through it many still meet the incomparable Christ, and they continue the testimony—"The only good thing about me is Christ!" Even though it took us a while to recognize it, Zawedde was the one. So are you. Your status, physical appearance, and personality are non-issues.

Character is an Issue—just a reminder lest we forget!

Spontaneity Takes Practice

You may have to convince yourself that spontaneity is okay, a good thing. Do you give yourself permission to seize a spur-of-the-moment opportunity, even if it disrupts your schedule? Can you make an impromptu visit? Do you graciously allow someone to drop in on you unannounced? Can you pray on the spot, whether in a church hallway, on a sidewalk, or at Walmart, with someone who shares a concern? Do abrupt changes in your schedule distress you? When did you last give away money in the twinkling of an eye without advance planning? Spontaneity and exuberance are cousins. Do you find exuberance acceptable or not? "Shout and be glad, O Daughter of Zion. For I am coming, declares the Lord," (Zechariah 2:10). Could you do that? Do you ever find that the wonder of the Lord overtakes the moment, and you rejoice with your whole being? Could such emotion appear on your face or display itself in your gait? Our world presses us into tight schedules with ungodly expectations of productivity and conformity. Such pressure squeezes both spontaneity and exuberance out of us. God would love to see them restored.

Simple actions can help you to break out of old patterns. Look people in the eye when speaking with them. Strive to remember names and faces. Speak to strangers, a compliment, or a comment on your shared situation, or a laugh on yourself. Be quick to do courtesies, such as opening doors, returning grocery carts, picking up dropped items or trash.

SMILE! Not only will you open yourself to God's assignments, but also you will help restore civility to our society. Let a harried shopper ahead of you in line, making eye and verbal contact. Next time you hear a need expressed, don't just commiserate, but also do something about it, without forming a committee.

Keep blank note cards handy, even in the car. Create personal folded calling cards with space to write a short note. Write brief notes of thanks and leave on desks for office mates. Tell people you are a praying person, and ask how you can pray for them—then be sure to do it.

Take a walk in the hallways of your office or in the mall, attempting to make smiling eye contact with five people in five minutes. When in a waiting room, don't pick up a magazine. Cruise the room visually and start a conversation. Share a table in a sandwich shop. Tell five people, "God has created a glorious morning," before you reach your desk. Eat lunch in a different spot. Travel a new route. Arrive early, or linger ten minutes longer. Don't use the drive-thru, rather go inside to eat, and concentrate on appearing approachable. Ask God to create an encounter.

These simple actions produce cracks in your well-ordered, pre-planned, over-stuffed day. You might find that you hear the Spirit's promptings more often, receive assignments in unexpected spots, and experience greater joy. These cracks make room for spontaneity, and joyful exuberance may show up too. These small alterations give God the opportunity to reveal his presence and his assignments. It takes practice.

and Preparation

Eugene Peterson, in his introduction to Thessalonians in *The Message*, writes as to how their concept of "the future sculpts the present," saying, "For if the future is dominated by the coming again of Jesus, there is little room left on the screen for projecting our anxieties and fantasies. It takes the clutter out of our lives. We're far more free to respond spontaneously to the freedom of God. . . . prodding us to continue to live forward in taut and joyful expectancy for what God will do next in Jesus."

We must de-clutter our schedules, our to-do-lists, our wish lists, and the anxieties and fantasies that clog our brains. We must create space in our lives for adequate response to God's assignments. If he asks us to invest in a person, we must have room to do so. Thom Rainer in *Simple Church* advises that we each participate in only one weekly worship service, one small group, and one ministry. Exhausted people are not spontaneous, nor even very useful. Opt out of some tasks. Move more slowly, and more intentionally. Rest in the Lord. Joy and exuberance give evidence of moving ahead well—living forward. Prepare and practice for spontaneity.

Energizers

Yet those who wait for the Lord will gain new strength.

Isaiah 40:31, NASB

Do you think living in daily sync with God takes more energy than you have?

Here are six areas in which waiting produces energy for the journey.

Engage with others in the Body

Join a church or smaller group within the church that enjoys spontaneous worship with song, prayer, Scripture, and praise. Regularly partake of the Lord's Supper with believers who hunger for holiness. Gather a group to pray through a book of Scripture, perhaps Colossians, looking for the Treasure. Find a few other church friends who will lay aside personal requests to pray God's heart for the world. As representatives of the body of Christ, go two by two and join a team or club: bird watching, public speaking, crafts, volleyball, after school mentoring, or whatever. Likewise, volunteer two-by-two for community service to touch people, unlike you. Ask someone to join you to read and discuss biographies of remarkable Christians, such as Moody, Brainard, Carmichael, Elliot, Fénelon, and Bonhoeffer. Ask God to give you a fellow breath-catcher for mutual encouragement and accountability. Then ask each other, "Where did you find God today?" Urge your church to schedule frequent personal testimonies of God's activity. Urge them to pray corporately for kingdom issues.

Engaging with the body takes time out of your schedule, more than a lone ranger life style would. God designed every function of his body, the church, to yield more than what we put into it. His people always accomplish more together than they can one by one. Grow to see participation in the body as waiting upon the Lord, and be amazed at the renewal of your energy.

Become a Seeker of Stories

Encourage people to tell you their story. Ask how the Lord drew them to himself, how he worked, blessed, and shaped. "Tell me about your journey to and with Christ." When you find a story, listen wholeheartedly, because it is God's story. Active listening helps you to see his footsteps, his moves, and to recognize him more quickly. Active listening with questions and comments helps the storyteller to recognize God in his own life. It helps him to acknowledge God's creative redemptive design upon his life—a great encouragement. Worship increases on all sides. So does energy.

Eugene Peterson's chapter on "Story-Making" in *Five Smooth Stones for Pastoral Work*—a profitable read—challenges all of us to take every person seriously by looking intently for God's story. This includes those far from God. Ask an acquaintance to tell you his story. Listen actively with interest and without judgment. Discernment will grow and God will work in the storytelling—perhaps giving you something of eternal significance to say or do.

Seeking and listening to stories can take a sizeable chunk out of your schedule. Consider this exercise as an opportunity to wait upon the Lord. I relate to you two events of finding a God-story in unlikely places. I assure you that I exited both events energized! God stories do that to us, regardless of the time consumed. Well worth the expenditure!

By the Grace of God

Since returning to Virginia in 2003, we've lived on a gravel road in the woods. A strong wind blew a walnut tree across the road, which a kind neighbor cut into pieces to clear our road. I scavenged a length containing a branch fork. After drying it a couple of years in a dark corner, I wanted it sawn into two-inch slabs. Driving up to a small mill not far from home, but hidden away at the end of an obscure road, I couldn't locate an employee. Eventually a man appeared, and we settled on the job. As he lifted the wood out of my trunk, he said, "I wouldn't be here except for the grace of God." Walking back into the mill and considering that statement, I felt prompted to say, "Sounds to me like you have a story to tell." Indeed he did. He shared a convoluted tale of misery and redemption for forty-five minutes. Worship rose to God from that hidden, obscure spot, much as the aroma of freshly cut lumber did. I thought this venture was simply about walnut slabs, but God amplified it.

Another Virginia venture involved eighteen months service on a grand jury investigating opiate abuse. My seat in the jury box placed me next to an older gentleman who had an impressive, resonating voice. During a break between witnesses, when we couldn't leave our seats, he turned and asked, "Have you been addicted to opiates?" A brief hesitation preceded my reply, "No." Another hesitation, then a prompting in my spirit led me to ask, "What about you? Have you suffered with addiction?" "Yes, I have." "How did you overcome it?" "By the grace of God . . ." His mellow, easy-to-listen to voice, blanketed the jury box as he told his story. He stepped into the lull and used me as his springboard. I thought this day would be spent enduring tragic opiate testimony, but God also intended a sermon of rescue and redemption for this grand jury of twenty. Indeed, that day was grand. Normally, after a jury day, exhaustion accompanied my forty-minute drive home but not this day. My eagerness to share with Jim the God-story banished exhaustion.

I know I told you there would be two Virginia stories of God's story, but I add another with a different twist. One summer, I frequented a small local plant nursery preparing for a major outdoor event. The same young lady assisted me, even coming to my home to offer advice. Two months into this project, a neighbor who followed the progress, realized that she knew this helpful nursery worker. Meeting her in town one day, my neighbor made the statement, "You know that Linda is a missionary, who worked in Africa?" The response: "NO! She can't be a missionary. She knows much of my story and I have never felt condemned." Learning of this response caused me catch my breath before the Lord. Two more months and countless conversations, the young lady became a joyful Christ-follower, much to her own amazement.

Practice Contemplation

Contemplation involves quiet, stillness, and meditation—all require unhurried time, waiting. Exercise the meditative side of life and you will find your walk invigorated, just as Isaiah 40:28-31 beautifully illustrates. Punctuate your life with days of solitude, devoted to the Word and prayer. Hear what Adele Ahlberg Calhoun in *Spiritual Disciplines Handbook* has to say on this topic.

We are hasty people bent on experiencing as much of life as we can. The faster we move, the more we can see, do, and produce. The more we network, the more options will be ours. The more options, the more living we can do …

But it is contemplation, not just having experiences, that truly opens us wide to life. Experiences can be lost to us in the mad rush to simply accumulate more. Contemplation invites us to enter in to the moment with a heart alive to whatever might happen. It is not just thinking about or analyzing an event or person. Contemplation asks us to see with faith, hope and love. It asks us to seek God and the "meanings" threaded through our days and years, so that our experience of being embedded in the triune life of God deepens and grows.

A contemplative person recognizes that every experience offers more than meets the eye. They know that "bidden or unbidden, God is present." Consequently contemplatives are open to seeing the unseen world … They enter into the being of life, alert to transcendencies in ordinary things. They believe God may be found and reverenced if one is prepared to notice how marvelously mysterious and personal life in this world is.[10]

Distinguish the difference between praying to God and experiencing God through prayer.

Examine biblical characters—Abraham, Jacob, Moses, Daniel, Hannah, Samuel, Job, Paul, and Jesus—as they pray. Work your way through the Psalms, turning them into prayer for your own life. The Bible is our prayer book. Read *Experiencing God through Prayer* by Madame Guyon, *The Practice of the Presence of God* by Brother Lawrence and *The Screwtape*

Letters by C.S. Lewis. Nurture an ongoing two-way dialogue with the Lord in the back of your head. Attach yourself to a prayer mentor. These practices cause attentiveness and anticipation to deepen. An amazing energy flows from that deep place. Well worth the wait!

Commit to being a Disciplined Disciple.

Live counter cultural. Opt for substantial diligence over a YouTube sound bite. Select one spiritual discipline—Sabbath keeping, simplicity, Bible study, solitude, confession, hospitality, or one of many others. Go deep into it. Research its historical use. Read past authors as well as living authors. Practice it deliberately. The tools of spiritual discipline mature the disciple. Helpful books: *Celebration of Discipline*, by Richard Foster, *Spirit of the Disciplines*, by Dallas Willard, and *Spiritual Disciplines Handbook: Practices That Transform Us* by Adele Ahlberg Calhoun. Exercise greater diligence in the Word and prayer than in any other activity, book, author, teaching program, or information source. As a disciplined disciple, train yourself to test everything by the Word. Determine to plant your feet on its solid ground, even as strange winds, fads, or insistent urges assail you, to blow you off balance. Synchronizing with God requires all your energy and strength. Live intentionally, not haphazardly. Don't squander your strength. Be a disciplined student, even though it takes time, so that you will use your energy wisely.

Expect surprise and mystery every day.

Sunday, July 4, 1976, when we lived in Mbale, a small town on the eastern side of Uganda, Doris came to my house for the weekend—a memorable one. Both our husbands had traveled out of the country for work assignments. That entire week was memorable. A hijacked Air France plane with 250 hostages aboard landed in Entebbe, Uganda, the previous Sunday. It originated from Tel Aviv, Israel. News and rumors were inseparable. Idi Amin's distressingly unpredictable role kept everyone on edge. During this week, a Ugandan Air Force friend overheard a discussion at the Entebbe airport, which named the hijacking's ringleader. He wanted to get this name to an outside authority. Unable to accomplish this himself, he came to Jim, the only expatriate he knew. Weighty discussions! America had no embassy in Uganda at that time. The decision reached involved an attempt to speak personally to the West German ambassador. Jim drove five hours to Kampala, through innumerable military road checks. I'm not sure who carried the heavier cloud that day, Jim or I. The German embassy staff allowed Jim to speak directly with the ambassador, who welcomed the information. Marvelous relief swept over me, as I saw our vehicle pull in the driveway the next day. We stayed close to home that week, not knowing what to expect.

Seven days into this drama, with both Jim and Doris' husband Harry away, Doris came to stay with me. Sunday morning, we decided to visit a church deep in the countryside, away from all the rumors and tension. The worship service, held outdoors against a dark brown mud-wall building covered with sky-blue morning glories, brilliant in the direct equatorial sun, soothed our souls. This drawing away into the heart of God, with his people, enabled us to enter into God's rest. Late that afternoon, turning onto our street, we met a large, boisterous crowd. This crowd surrounded our house, covered the yard, and spilled out into the road. We inched our Land Rover through the people toward the driveway. One man shouted out, "If I could find an Israeli, I'd give him a goat to feast with!" Israeli commandos had rescued the hostages while we worshiped in the village. We Rices were the only foreign people in town. So naturally, this spontaneous party gravitated to our house, gathering to celebrate. Our personal jubilation dissipated quickly. This celebration rejoiced not only in the release of hostages but also in the defeat and humiliation of President Amin. Realizing the danger, we sent everyone away as fast as possible. Indeed, that night Ugandans across the nation died in similar celebrations as the army retaliated.

We lived that chaotic week moment by moment in high drama. Did Jim's information prove helpful? Did the timing of our return home save lives? I'm glad God doesn't show us the big picture, or even tomorrow for that matter. I might flee or at least stay in bed and bury my head under the pillows. In order to thrive in the midst of our daily drama, we must nurture anticipation for the unexpected and rest joyfully amazed, rather than forlornly dismayed, as it unfolds. God does have a plan for order, even amid our chaos. Remember, God is the One who created the earth from emptiness and nothing. He can do a good job with this day too.

Dismay exhausts. We could have lived that week in forlorn dismay, voicing our "woe is me" every step of the way. We could have poured our God-given energy out onto the ground, wasting its fruitfulness. But we did not, thanks to the grace of God. We walked through that week with anticipation that God would show up; how he would appear we didn't know. I admit that some of those anticipation hours were tense. That tension added eagerness to our expectation without throwing us into despair, and without robbing us of our joy. Joy energizes. The same God who had Isaiah write 40:31, "Those who wait for the Lord will gain new strength," also dictated to Nehemiah in verse 8:10, "The joy of the Lord is your strength." Beware of dismay as an energy-sapping tool of Satan. Allow the mystery and surprise of his ways to enhance anticipation and joy. Choose joy—yes, it is a choice—rather than dismay if you desire the necessary energy to live for kingdom building. God designed you for this.

Urgency is Real

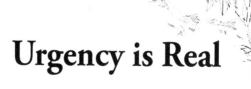

Making the most of every opportunity...

Ephesians 5:16

Read the flying scroll vision in Zechariah 5:1-4. I suspect you've had dreams of weirder things. This vision differs from our sleep dreams, as Zechariah, fully awake, dialogued with an angel, asking and answering questions. They saw a scroll, a common object for Jews, although a huge one, thirty by fifteen feet in size. It flew in the sky overhead. The angel described it as a curse traveling to find its recipient.

Ugandans understand curses. They can pay a witchdoctor to invoke a curse on an enemy or a disliked relative. Also, they can pay the same person to revoke a troubling curse, which some disgruntled neighbor or deceased ancestor may have initiated. Witchdoctors utilize bones, herbs, aromas, things buried in the ground, tossed upon a roof, or sewn into the seams of garments. They do have power, and they exercise great influence. This flying scroll vision speaks to Ugandans.

An inscription on each side of the flying scroll identified the curses' recipients. These two indictments named, on one side, those who sinned against man, and on the other side, those who sinned against God. When the scroll found such a person, it flew into his house and quietly waited—waiting for the moment of fulfillment. It waits because God desires that none should perish by this curse. He restrains the curse and waits, hoping for repentance. Read 2 Peter 3: 9-10.

However, he doesn't wait forever. A time comes when, as in Zechariah 6:7, God says, "Go throughout the earth!" His command releases the devastation of the curse. This scroll has spent a night in the house hidden, but when the command comes, it destroys the house, its timbers, and its stones. Picture a van full of explosives parked alongside a police station, or a suicide bomber mingling with a crowd in a market. The explosive's detonator, linked to a cell phone, awaits a call. When it comes, destruction, devastation, and death explode upon the scene.

Luzira Prison, outside of Kampala, bulged with prisoners—some criminal, some political, and some just found in the wrong place at the wrong time. Condemned prisoners filled Luzira's death row. Perhaps you've seen pictures of a third-world prison—definitely not a hygienic, well-oiled machine. God had chosen an enthusiastic man, William, to preach the gospel inside this prison. William invited me to speak to the condemned prisoners. (Whenever we met, he spoke of my gray hair as a crown of glory, so how could I refuse his invitation?) Walking through those notorious doors, I confess to some trepidation. Hundreds of men crowded into a barren courtyard. I taught the flying scroll vision, using a paper scroll to demonstrate. These condemned men clearly understood curses, and they considered themselves cursed. They blamed deceased ancestors, traditional tribal enemies, the wealthy, disgruntled wives, opposition politicians, foreigners, and even their own children. The flying scroll graphically portrayed a new understanding as to the true source of their curse. "The wages of sin is death," Romans 6:23. Verses from

Galatians revealed the way of escape, counteracting the curse, nullifying its mission.

Read Galatians 3:10-14. Scripture tells us that Christ on the cross took the curse meant for us onto his own body, and absorbed its explosion. For all who have chosen to follow and live like Christ, Christ delivers you from the curse. For all who have chosen to walk away from Christ, the curse remains, lying silent in their house, awaiting its time of detonation—the Day of Judgment. Allow this image to knead urgency into your priorities, your schedules. Allow it to work as yeast in your life. Is the flying scroll under your neighbor's bed? Is it in the basement of your brother? Is it lying under a co-worker's workstation? Allow the Holy Spirit to amplify this vision in your imagination. Listen intently to *hear* its message. You will de-clutter, act more spontaneously, and have greater awareness of the kingdom of God. "Making the most of every opportunity" takes on sharper meaning and influences priorities. This flying scroll vision compels us to accept God-given assignments consistently—amazed at their frequency and their profitability.

One Last Story

You have already read the story of my second carjacking. Let me tell of the first. Driving home mid-afternoon, alone, I exited a major roundabout. Moving uphill, I came to a wide, deep pothole, which wasn't uncommon in those days. I slowed to drive into the hole, and as I drove across it, a vehicle whipped around me and pulled diagonally in front of me. Four men in camouflage military uniforms jumped out. All four pointed AK-47s at me—two through the windshield and one through each side window. At this point, my feet and brain disconnected, refusing to coordinate in the attempt to stop the straight-shift car. The vehicle and I lurched. A soldier jerked open my door and shoved me to the center. My mind gasped, "They plan to take me with them!" He stopped the car and tossed me out just beyond the shoulder of the road. In a heap in the dust, I'm elated. "They don't plan to take me!" Before I completed that thought, I was grabbed from behind by my shoulders and yanked upright. They had noticed my purse, which still hung on my shoulder. Yanking away the purse, they threw me back into the dust, and sped off.

This event probably took less time than it took you to read the previous paragraph. But in that brief juncture, a crowd gathered. Crowds of people covered the city roads, all day. (Kristen, on her first stay in America, puzzled by the vacant sidewalks asked, "Where are all the people in America?") These carjacking witnesses pressed in close and asked, "Are you okay? Are you hurt? Aren't you terrified? What are you going to do now? Who are you? Where do you come from?" "I'm okay. It happened too quickly for terror to get a solid grip. I came from America, and I will walk home." That dense clot of a crowd moved with me. At least fifty people followed and kept asking questions. "Why are you in Kampala? What do you do? Are you going to leave now?" "I have come to introduce people to Jesus. I teach the Bible and help churches grow. No, I'm not leaving." "Why would you stay?" "God called me with my husband to come. I won't leave because of a bad event, because of wicked people. Only the gospel goodness of God can deal with evil. Jesus overcomes evil with his goodness. He is the hope that we all need these days …" And so the conversation went. That crowd walked with me all the way home, a distance of about one mile. We took up the road as well as the sidewalk. They stopped at my gate, thanking me profusely for coming to Uganda and for staying with them,

Thirty minutes earlier, I lay in a heap in the dust, and now I walked on air, praising God for his amazing capacity to use any moment for his glory. Those fifty people heard the Gospel, and God allowed me to tell them. He is amazing, breath-catchingly so.

From the first instance of our existence to the last,

God has never assigned us a barren moment.[1]

Francois Fénelon

He Calls You Through Zechariah

You've gotten the measures wrong.

You see illusions.

My wall of fire surrounds you,
My robe of righteousness clothes you,
My Spirit, My glory, pours forth to fill you.

Do you not know the Lord Almighty sent Me to you?

I came humble on a donkey, sold, pierced, abandoned.
I burn with jealously for you.
You are the apple of My eye,
You are the sparkling gemstone in my hand,
Even your cooking pots are holy to Me.

Do you not know the Lord Almighty sent Me to you?

I have chosen you again and again and again.
My anger burns against those who stole you from Me.
Come out of Babylon. You don't belong there. Flee!
Return to Me so that I may return to you
I whistle loud and clear into your distant place.

Do you not know the Lord Almighty sent Me to you?

I am coming. I will dwell in your midst. Shout for joy.
Catch your breath! Be still before the Lord Almighty.
He is aroused from His holy habitation.
He rises to speak, to act.
Remember Me.

What do you see? Look! What do you hear? Listen!

Catch Your Breath

Acknowledgements

As I wrote, the influence of Eugene Peterson became obvious. For many years, my husband Jim supplied me with Peterson's books, to nourish my spiritual life. Starting in the mid '80s, Jim gave me *Earth and Altar* where I was surprised to find a *living* author who held such a high view of prayer. From then on, I was hooked. You who have read Peterson will recognize his influence. I owe much to both Jim and Eugene Peterson.

Likewise, I acknowledge Henry Blackaby for the useful tool *Experiencing God*. In every assignment locale, his material proved Spirit ordained. You might wonder why I wrote this book, as it is similar in some ways. I wrote for those who didn't quite get it, those who didn't reach the last chapter, those who won't sit though a workbook class, and for those who learn by doing and seeing. I don't want any to miss the *Experiencing God* message, so I've repackaged it hoping to entice yet others to taste and see that the Lord is good.

Missionary colleague Linda Listrom and friend Iris Layman worked on the illustrations. Jim, Diane, Kristen, and Mom enthusiastically supported the process. Thanks go to Vie Herlocker who opened my eyes to grammar, punctuation, and tight writing. How so many people could have such debates over my commas, I may never fathom.

Endnotes:

1. Francois Fénelon, *The Best of Fénelon*, edited by Harold Chadwick, (Gainesville, FL: Bridge-Logos Publishers, 2002), p. 102

2. Os Guinness, *The Call* (Nashville, TN: Word Publishing, 1998), p. 4

3. Eugene Peterson, *Take and Read* (Grand Rapids/Cambridge: Wm B. Eerdmans and Vancouver, B. C.: Regent College, 2000), p. xiii

4. Emilie Griffin, editor, *The Cloud of Unknowing*, (San Francisco: HarperSanFrancisco, 1981), p. 10

5. Emilie Griffin, editor, T*he Cloud of Unknowing*, (San Francisco: HarperSanFrancisco, 1981), p. 10

6. Os Guinness, *The Call* (Nashville, TN: Word Publishing, 1998), p. 24

7. Oswald Chambers, *My Utmost for His Highest* (Westwood, NJ: Barbour & Company, 1963) p. 86

8. Os Guinness, *The Call* (Nashville, TN: Word Publishing, 1998), p. 68

9. O. Hallesby, *Under His Wings* (Minneapolis, MN: Augsburg, 1945) pp. 104-105

10. Adele Ahlberg Calhoun, *Spiritual Disciplines Handbook: Practices That Transform Us* (Downers Grove, Ill.: InterVarsity Press, 2005), p. 49

CPSIA information can be obtained
at www.ICGtesting.com
Printed in the USA
LVHW040132091020
668359LV00014B/838

9 780984 551590